Charts & Publications

Navigational Charts

A chart catalogue shows the coverage of available charts and their respective catalogue numbers.

Electronic charts can be displayed on a dedicated plotter or a PC. Updates for some types are available, making them easy to correct. Be aware that the quality, detail and coverage of electronic charts varies widely.

Small-craft folios usually contain 10 or more charts designed for use on small-craft chart tables. Many popular sailing areas are covered around the world.

Keep your charts up to date by making minor corrections. Details of these are found in Hydrographic Office 'Notices to Mariners'.

You may have to replace a chart if major corrections are needed. Usually a new edition of a chart is produced instead.

Nautical Almanacs and Pilot Books

Publications giving notes on pilotage can greatly enhance the information gleaned from a chart. They can give aerial photographs, detailed pilotage notes and sketches, local information/town plans etc. Be aware that information from pilotage publications can be out of date and is not a substitute for a fully corrected chart.

Small-craft almanacs give a large amount of extremely useful information, such as tidal heights and streams, pilotage and passage-planning information, and weather information.

CHARTS & PUBLICATIONS

Geodetic Datums

Latitude and longitude from a GNSS is a reference to a geodetic datum, which is a theoretical model of the earth. Historically, each national hydrographic office developed their own datum for their charts. As the world is not a perfect sphere, each datum will have areas where they match the earth's shape well and areas where they do not.

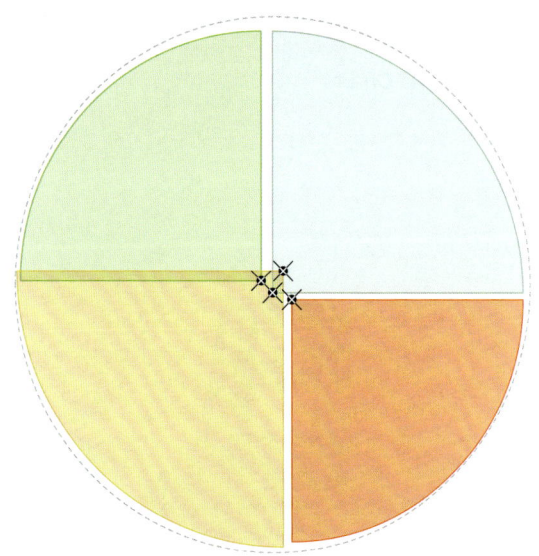

GNSS introduced a new problem in that the position expressed by the latitude and longitude in a GNSS system does not automatically match the datum of the printed chart you are plotting on. By default, GNSS systems plot against a datum called WGS84, and charts have gradually moved to adopt this standard.

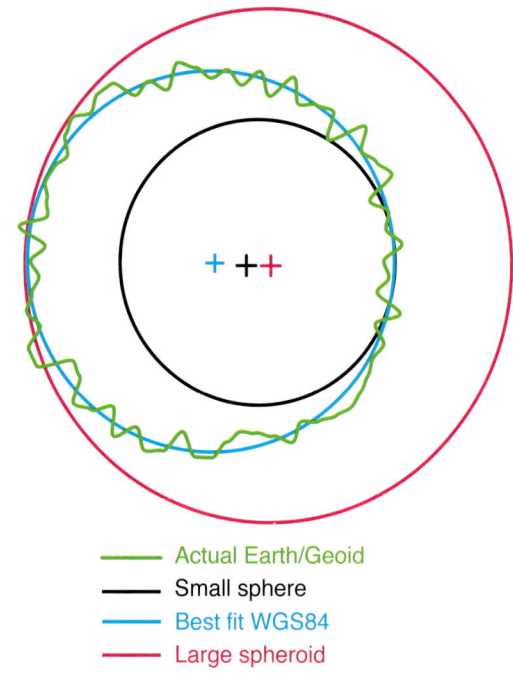

— Actual Earth/Geoid
— Small sphere
— Best fit WGS84
— Large spheroid

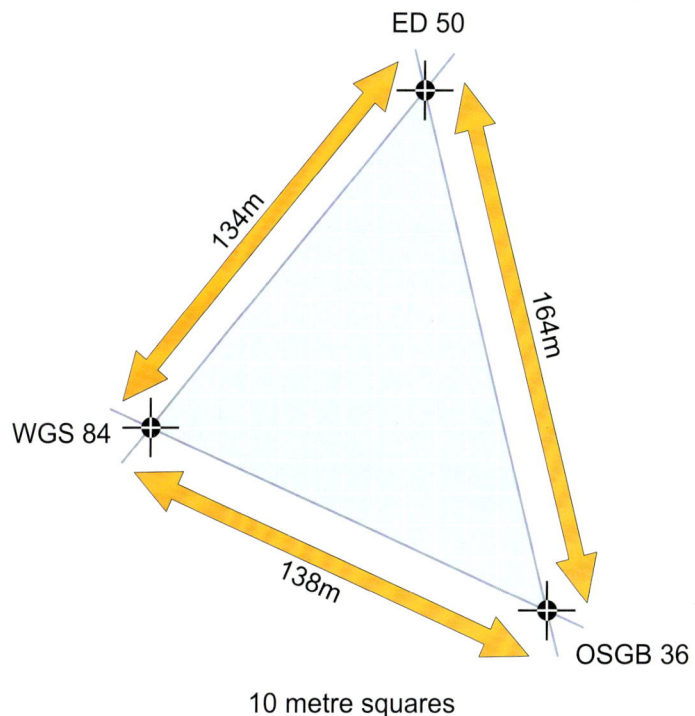

10 metre squares

The three plots show how a position in the Dover Strait can differ if plotted on different datums. In some areas the wrong datum can give errors of over a mile. Charts will always declare their datum and any corrections to be added to WGS84 positions prior to plotting.

Chart Projection

Chart projections are an attempt to represent the curved surface of the earth on a flat piece of paper.

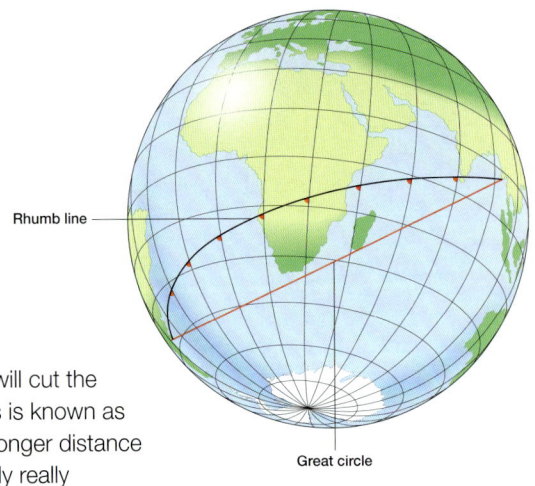

The shortest distance between two points on the earth's surface is on a great-circle route.

If you sail an unchanging course you will cut the lines of longitude at equal angles. This is known as a rhumb line route. You sail a slightly longer distance using a rhumb line route but this is only really significant on a long ocean passage.

The most useful chart for practical use is one where a rhumb line is shown as a straight line.

Mercator Projection

In order to represent a rhumb line as a straight line the meridians have to be made parallel. This stretches land masses at the top of a chart in an east-west direction, so to keep them the correct shape they must also be stretched in a north-south direction.

The scale gradually increases towards the top of the chart. This is why you must always measure distance on the latitude scale opposite your position.

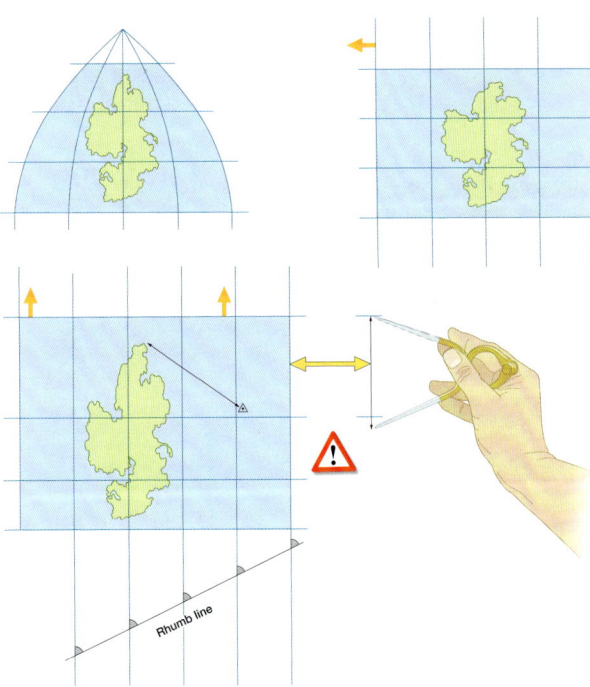

CHART PROJECTION

Mercator projections are used for passage-making charts for coastal and offshore passages. Distances are measured in sea miles using the latitude scale closest to your position. Over larger areas there is a noticeable difference in the size of a sea mile from the top to the bottom of the chart.

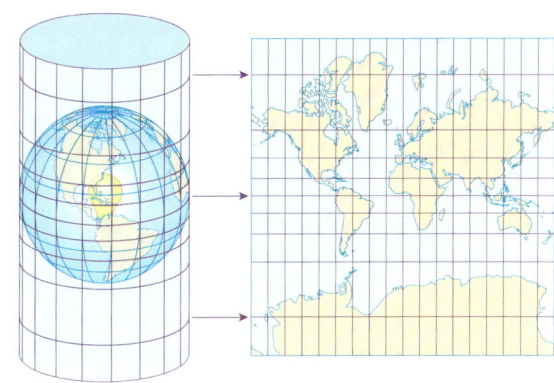

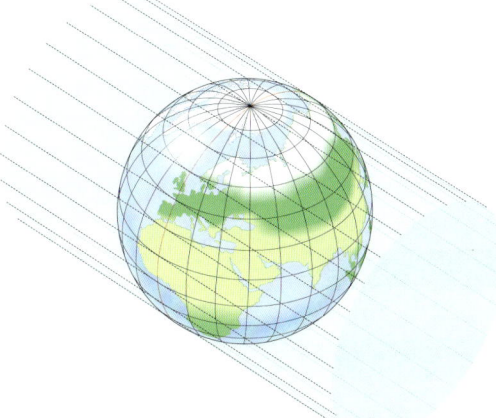

Transverse mercator projections are commonly used in large-scale harbour plans as they allow for accurate distance and bearing measurements over small areas.

Gnomonic Projection

This projection is mainly used for planning ocean passages, as a great-circle route is shown as a straight line.

As the charted area moves further from the centre of the projected area (the tangential point), greater distortion takes place. So, a typical ocean-planning chart will have its tangential point in the centre of the charted area.

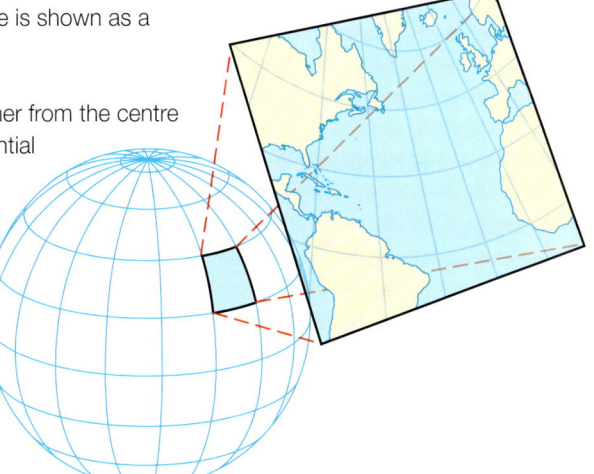

CHART PROJECTION

Distance

1 degree latitude = 60' (minutes)

1' = 60" (seconds)

1 minute of latitude = 1 sea mile.

We use tenths of a minute, not seconds for chartwork e.g. 50°17'.4N.

The length of a sea mile varies slightly with latitude so for practical purposes we use the nautical mile, which is fixed in length.

Although the sea mile varies in size depending on latitude it can be used as an approximation of a nautical mile for offshore and coastal passage making.

A knot is one nautical mile per hour.

1 kilometre
1000m

1 statute (land) mile
1609m

1 nautical mile
1852m

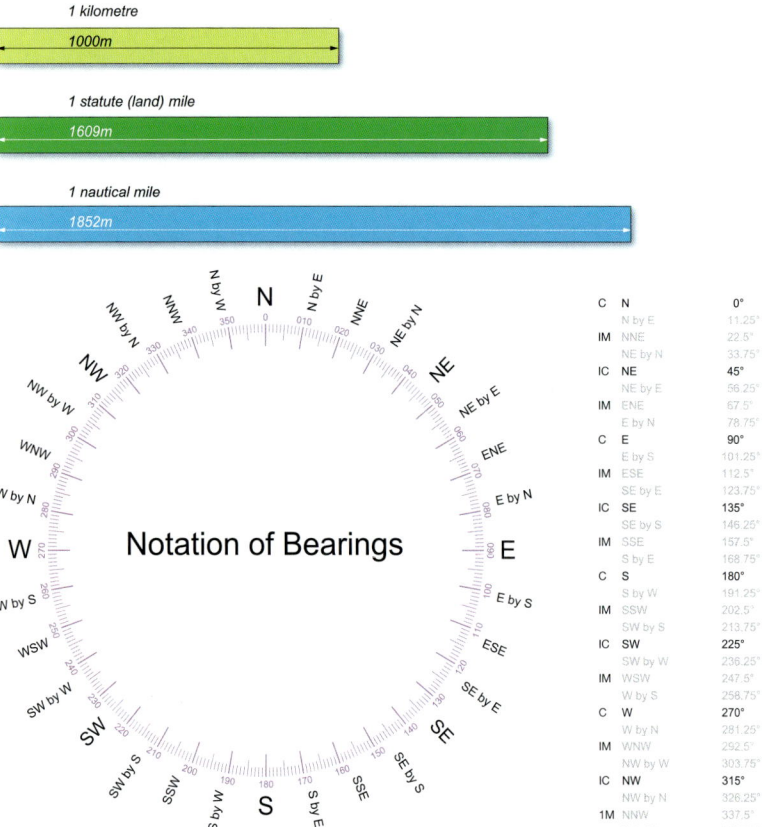

C	N	0°
	N by E	11.25°
IM	NNE	22.5°
	NE by N	33.75°
IC	NE	45°
	NE by E	56.25°
IM	ENE	67.5°
	E by N	78.75°
C	E	90°
	E by S	101.25°
IM	ESE	112.5°
	SE by E	123.75°
IC	SE	135°
	SE by S	146.25°
IM	SSE	157.5°
	S by E	168.75°
C	S	180°
	S by W	191.25°
IM	SSW	202.5°
	SW by S	213.75°
IC	SW	225°
	SW by W	236.25°
IM	WSW	247.5°
	W by S	258.75°
C	W	270°
	W by N	281.25°
IM	WNW	292.5°
	NW by W	303.75°
IC	NW	315°
	NW by N	326.25°
IM	NNW	337.5°
	N by W	348.75°

C = Cardinal   IM = Intermediate   IC = Intercardinal

Magnetic Variation

Charts show North as True (geographic) North. Gyro compasses point to True North but are rare on small vessels due to the cost, and the need for a steady power supply. Most small vessels carry magnetic compasses, which point to Magnetic North. The different between True North and Magnetic North at any one location is called variation.

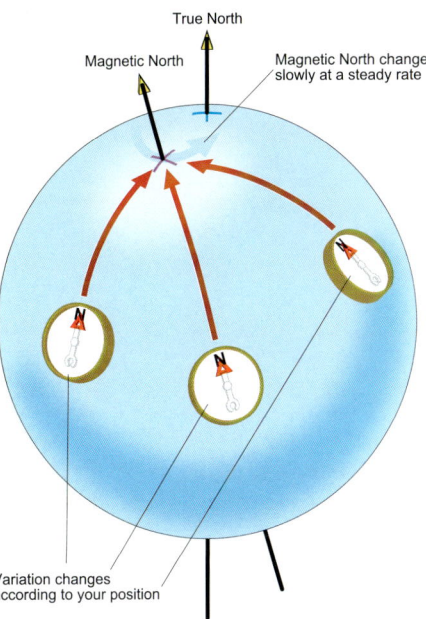

Here, the variation is reducing by a few minutes each year. Variation in Canada, South Africa and New Zealand can be over 20 degrees. The rate of change is shown on the compass rose.

Bearings on a chart are shown in degrees True, so you must apply variation to bearings from and to the chart.

Example – variation 7°W

090° True
+7° West Variation
097° Magnetic

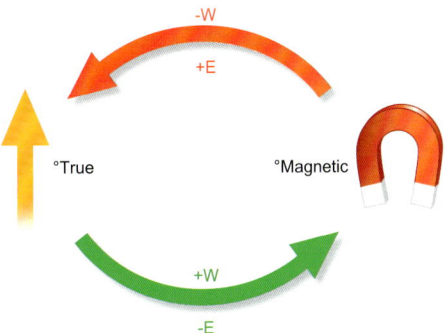

[9]

Compass Deviation

Ferrous metal and magnetic fields (for instance the engine, instruments, cockpit speakers and mobile phones) will affect the compass.

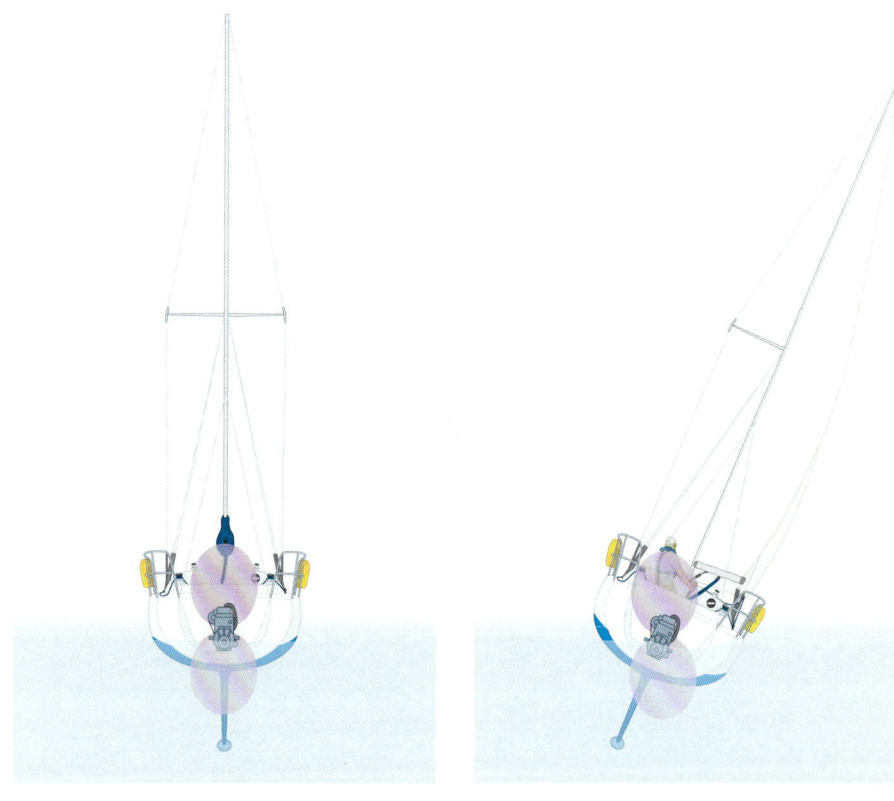

As the boat heels, the influences change.

COMPASS DEVIATION

Deviation Card

A deviation card can be produced for your steering compass which will show the east or west error on each heading. Use this to convert from °C to °M and vice versa.

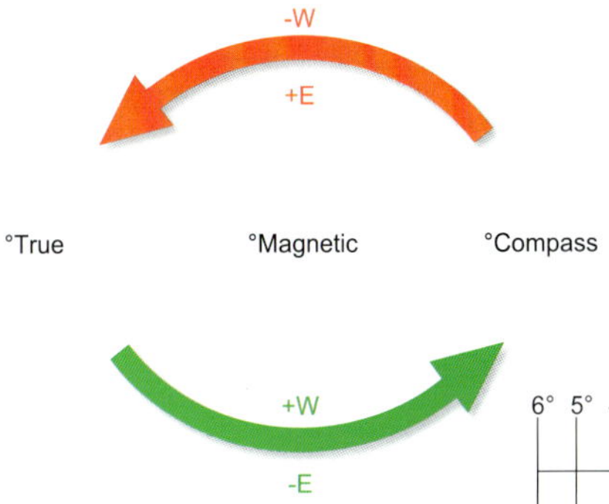

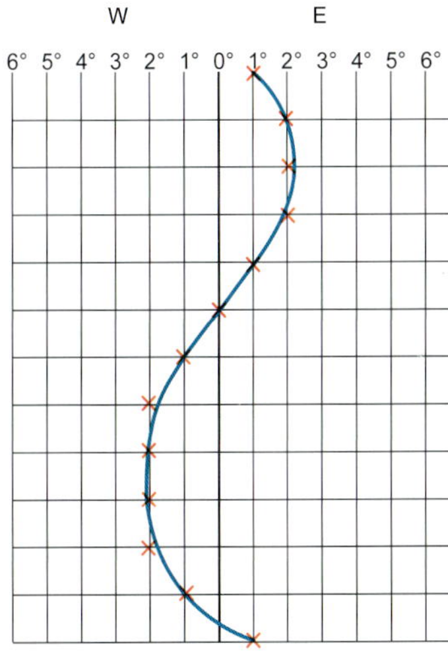

°True   °Magnetic   °Compass

Ship's heading °(Compass)	Deviation
000°	1°E
030°	2°E
060°	2°E
090°	2°E
120°	1°E
150°	0°
180°	1°W
210°	2°W
240°	2°W
270°	2°W
300°	2°W
330°	1°W
000°	1°E

Practical Application

It is preferable to have your steering compass corrected to eliminate deviation. However, you may be on an unfamiliar boat, such as a charter boat, or on a delivery trip. In this situation it is always wise to check for deviation and apply it as necessary.

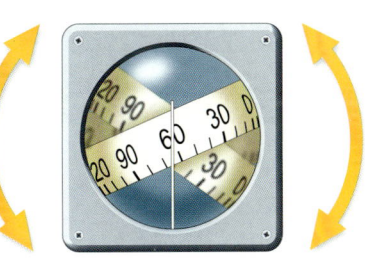

Be aware that even in a moderate sea it is difficult to steer a very precise course. This means you may decide to ignore small amounts of deviation.

If you find that your compass has developed a significant deviation error then you should have it adjusted by an experienced compass adjuster.

Tidal Theory

The gravitational interaction of the earth with the sun and moon causes the tidal cycles we experience.

There are three distinct elements in the roughly monthly cycles.

The Lunar Cycle (Average of 29.53 Days' Cycle)

Spring Tides
When the gravitational pulls from the moon and the sun are in line, we experience:
- high high waters
- low low waters.

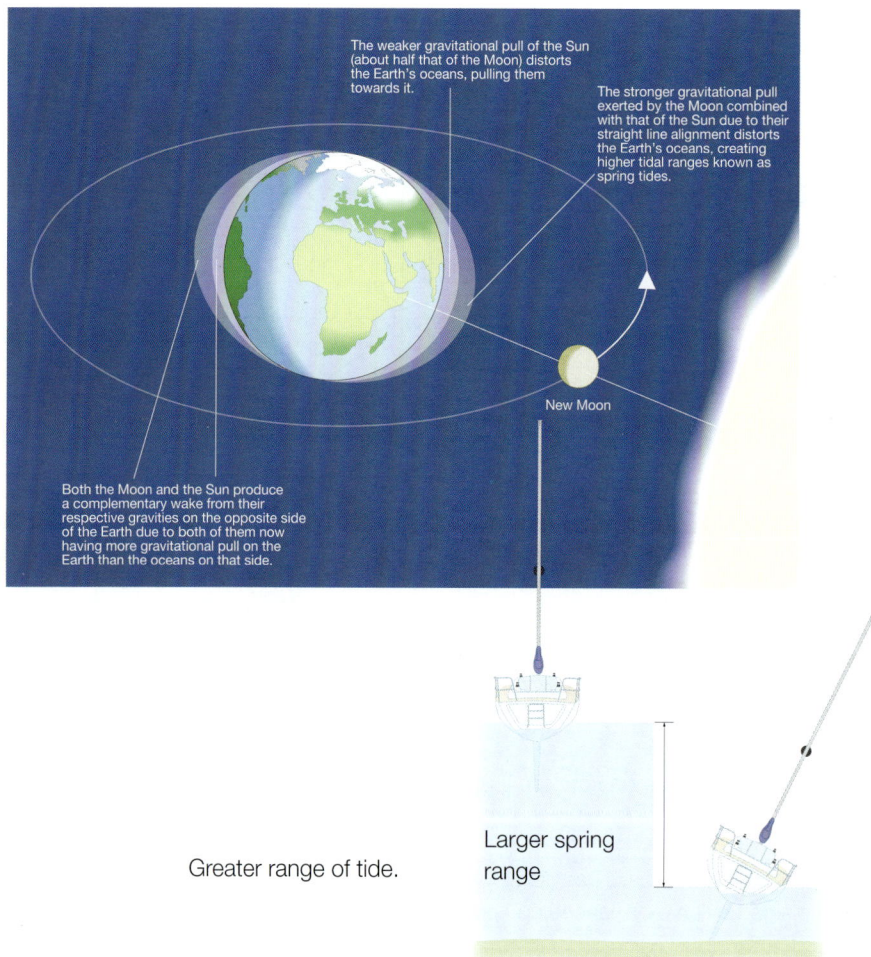

TIDAL THEORY

Neap Tides

When the gravitational pulls from the moon and the sun are at right angles to each other, we experience:
- low high waters
- high low waters.

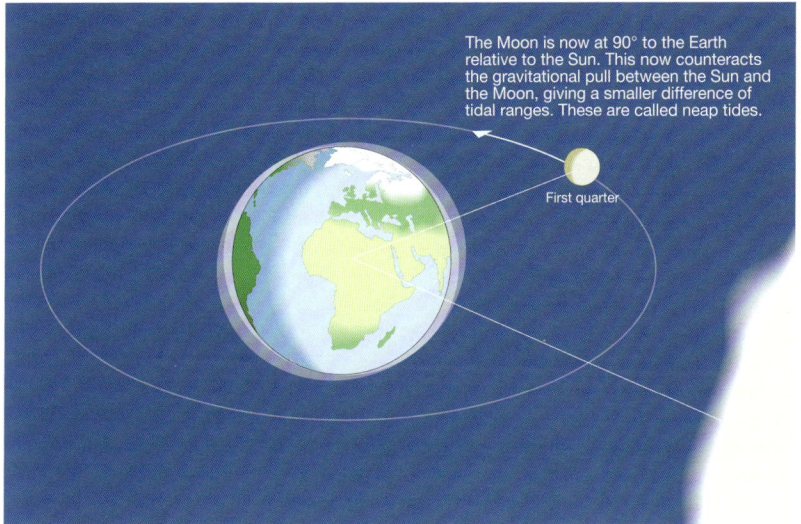

Smaller range of tide.

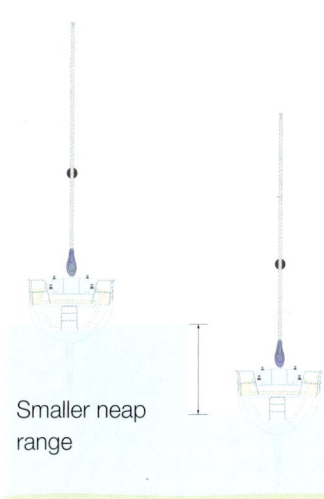

TIDAL THEORY

Declination

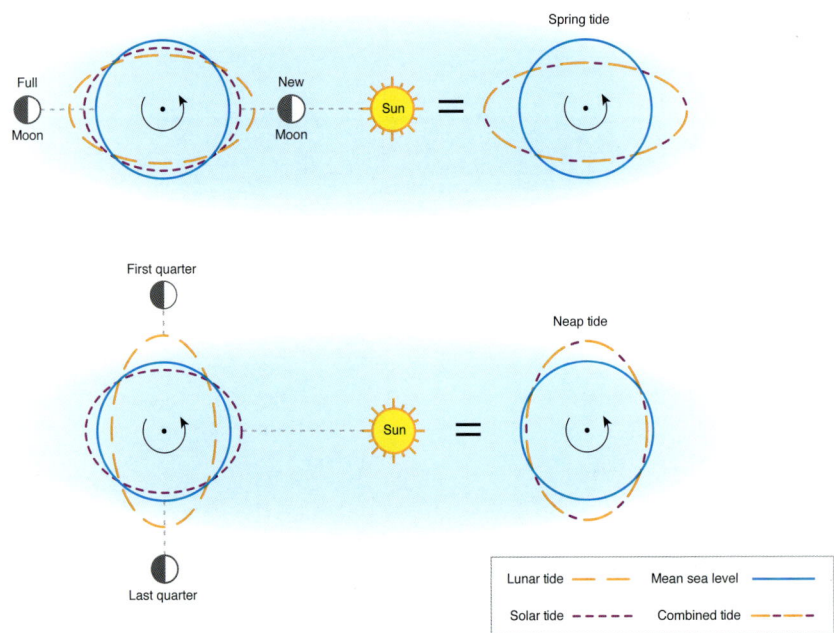

The Moon's Declination (Average of 27.21 Days)

When the moon's declination (its height above the celestial equator) is high an inequality in tidal height occurs within the daily cycle. Points X and Y represent the same geographic location on the earth's surface 12 hours apart. X has a noticeably smaller height of HW.

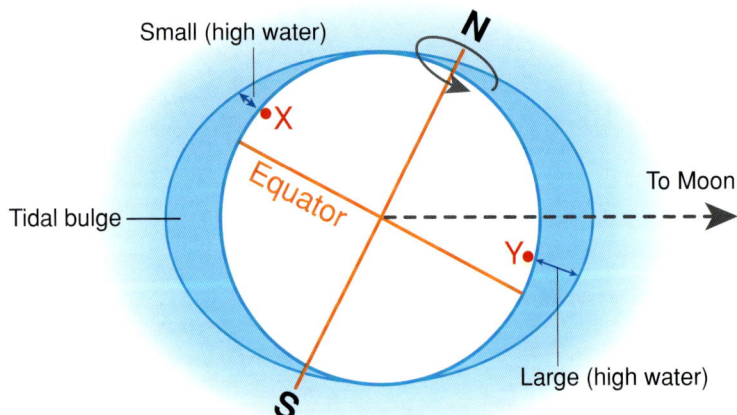

TIDAL THEORY

The Perigee-Apogee Cycle (Average of 27.55 Days)

The moon's orbit is not uniform and it has a perigee (the point when it is closest to the earth), where its effect is most powerful, and an apogee (when it is furthest away from the earth), where it is least powerful. The illustration shows the effect of this cycle on the range of two spring tides. The largest part is when the moon was in perigee.

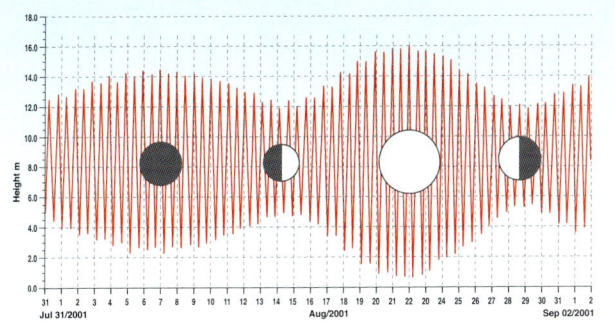

Global Patterns

Tidal patterns round the world are quite complex due to the effects of:
- funnelling, e.g. into the mouth of the Bristol Channel
- the spin of the earth
- the differing geography of ocean basins
- shallow water.

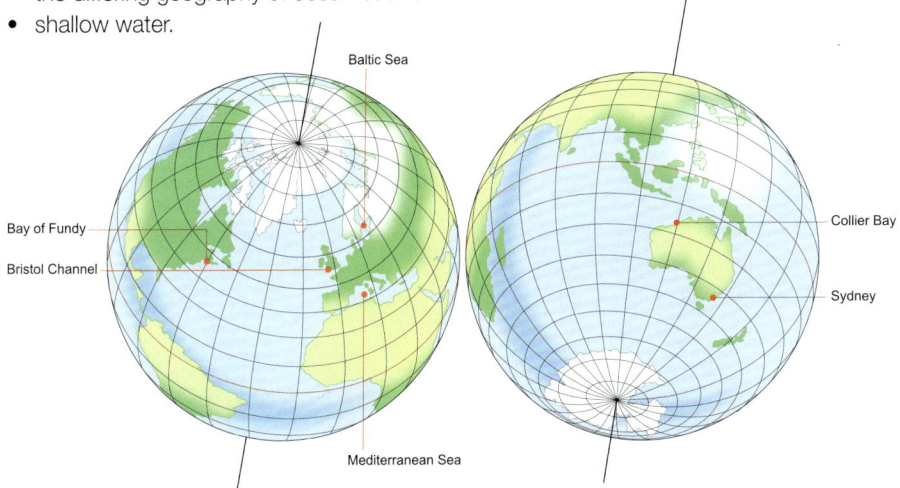

The biggest tidal range in the world is in Canada in the Bay of Fundy (mean range 13m). The second biggest is in the Bristol Channel (12m). Range differs within a country. Collier Bay on the north-west coast of Australia has a mean spring range over 10m, whereas the south-east coast has just a 1–3m range.

The Mediterranean and Baltic seas have negligible tides, mainly because of restrictions at their entrance.

[15]

TIDAL THEORY

■ Semidiurnal tides ■ Diurnal tides ■ Mixed tides

Not all areas have the same tidal cycle. Some have two comparable cycles per day (semidiurnal), some have one cycle per day (diurnal), while others have two cycles which are significantly different in each day (mixed).

TIDAL THEORY

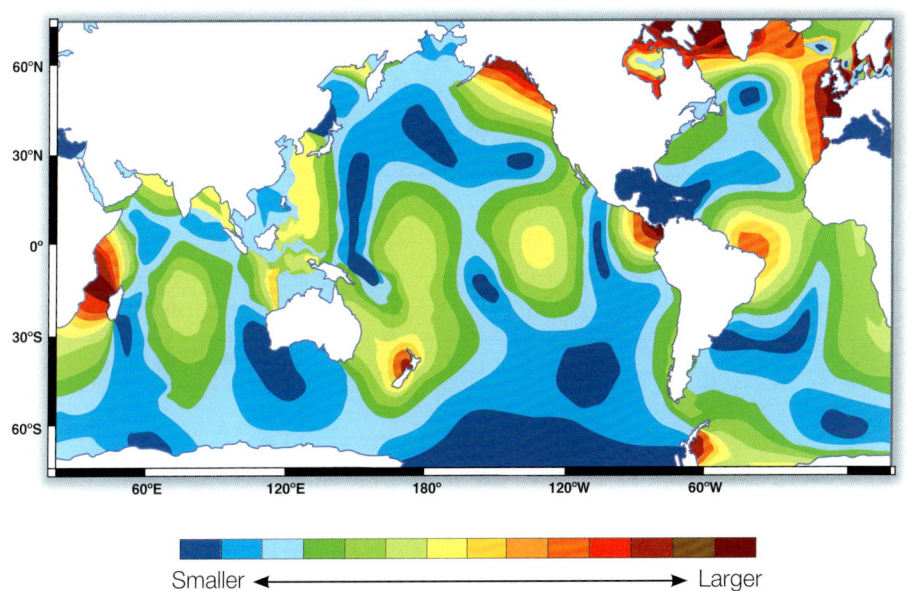

The tidal range varies around the globe.

TIDAL THEORY

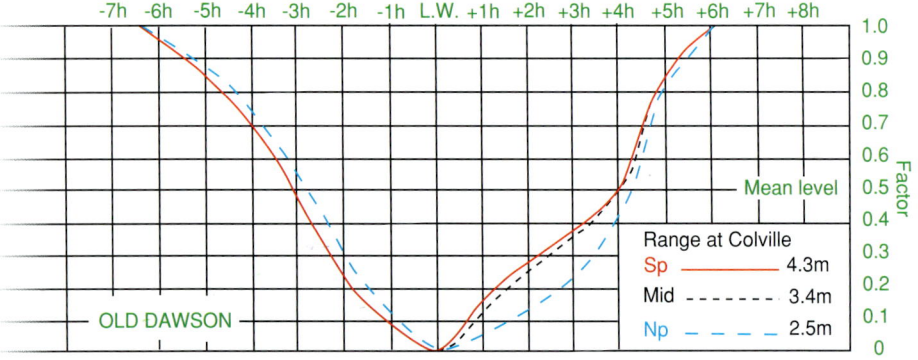

It is important to remember that tidal predictions are just predictions from some form of computer model. An example to reinforce this is the inverted tidal curve – in some areas predicting the time of HW accurately is sufficiently difficult that tidal curves have to be based on the times of low water.

TIDAL THEORY

Effects of the Weather

Strong winds for prolonged periods can:
- Hold water back, making the tidal height greater than predicted
- Push water out, making the tidal height less than predicted.

Barometric pressure can:
- Make the tidal height less than predicted
- Make the tidal height greater than predicted.

Tidal Terms

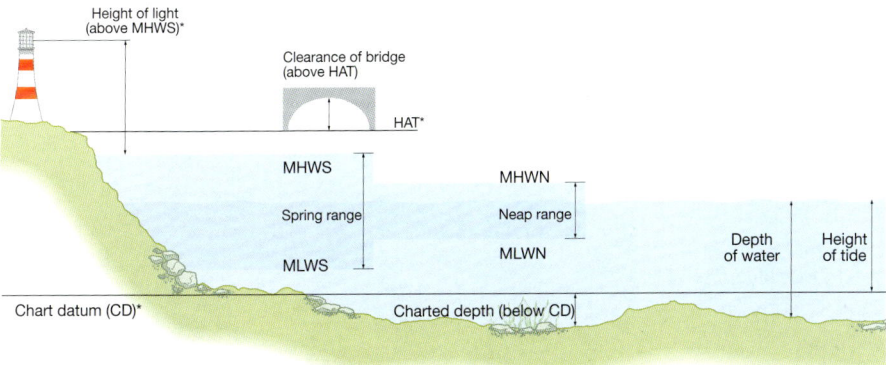

*Specific datums used for heights, clearances, and charted depth may vary in different countries. For example, the UK uses lowest astronomical tide for chart datum, whereas the USA uses mean low low water.

[19]

Tidal Curves (Standard Ports)

Tide tables are produced for larger ports and give the times and heights of high and low water for every day of the year. Tide times may need correcting for local changes, such as differences in time zone from Universal Time (UT) and in countries operating Daylight Saving Time (DST) in the summer (BST in the U.K.).

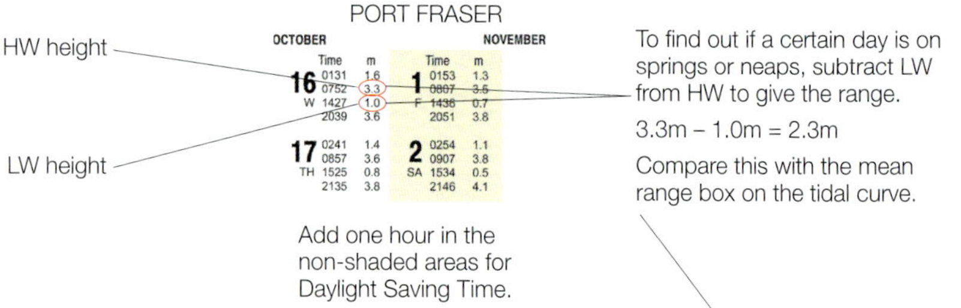

PORT FRASER

OCTOBER			NOVEMBER		
	Time	m		Time	m
16	0131	1.6	**1**	0153	1.3
	0752	3.3		0807	3.5
W	1427	1.0	F	1436	0.7
	2039	3.6		2051	3.8
17	0241	1.4	**2**	0254	1.1
	0857	3.6		0907	3.8
TH	1525	0.8	SA	1534	0.5
	2135	3.8		2146	4.1

HW height — (3.3 circled)
LW height — (1.0 circled)

Add one hour in the non-shaded areas for Daylight Saving Time.

To find out if a certain day is on springs or neaps, subtract LW from HW to give the range.

3.3m − 1.0m = 2.3m

Compare this with the mean range box on the tidal curve.

TIDAL CURVES

Use these for finding out depth of water at any time between high and low water.

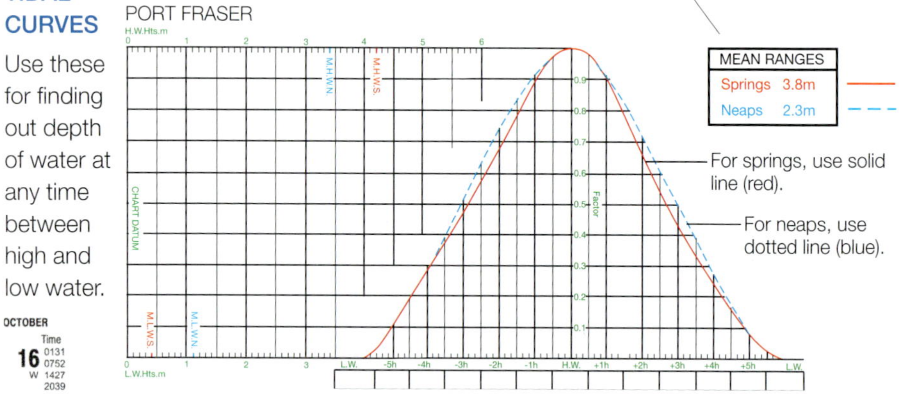

PORT FRASER

MEAN RANGES
Springs 3.8m
Neaps 2.3m

For springs, use solid line (red).

For neaps, use dotted line (blue).

OCTOBER
Time
16 0131
0752
W 1427
2039

Being able to predict tidal height within the tidal cycle will enable you to identify safe times of entry and departure to drying harbours, or harbours which have drying approaches or sills.

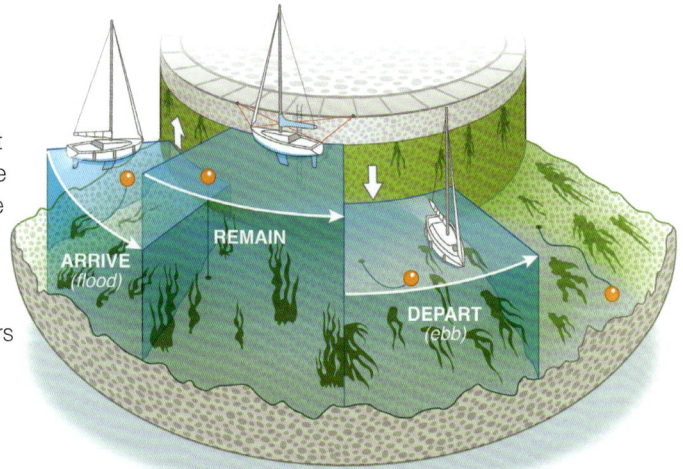

ARRIVE *(flood)*
REMAIN
DEPART *(ebb)*

Secondary Ports

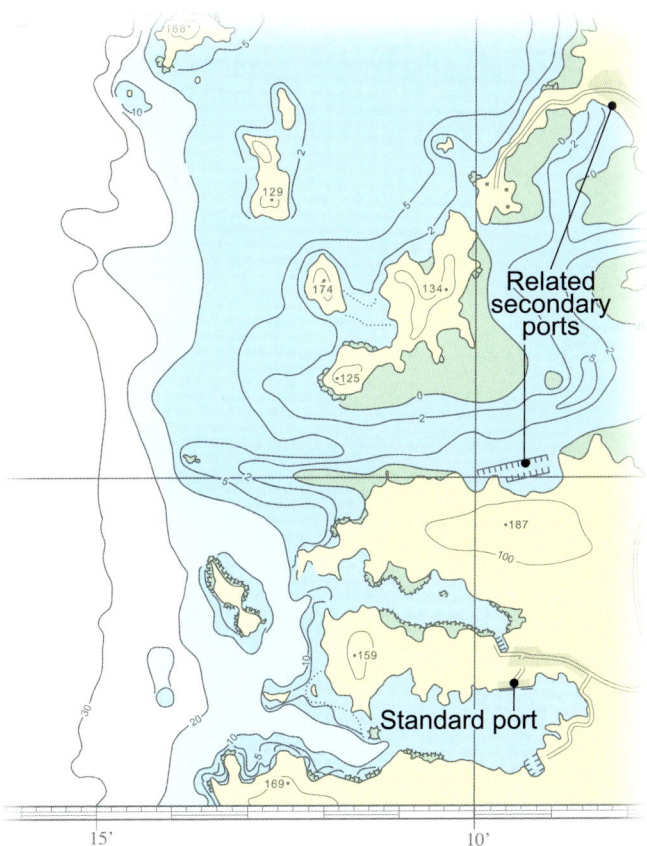

Small ports may produce their own tide tables, but almanacs and official tide tables include adjustments that can be applied to the times and heights of standard ports to work out the correct information for secondary ports.

Standard Port PORT FRASER (←)

Times				Height (metres)			
High Water		Low Water		MHWS	MHWN	MLWN	MLWS
0000	0600	0500	1100	4.2	3.4	1.1	0.4
1200	1800	1700	2300				

Differences ROZELLE COVE

-0038	-0018	-0036	-0014	+0.2	-0.2	+0.5	+0.2

Secondary Port Calculations

Rozelle Cove

Find the time and height of HW and LW on Wednesday 24 April.

Standard Port PORT FRASER (←)

Times		Height (metres)					
High Water		Low Water		MHWS	MHWN	MLWN	MLWS
0000	0600	0500	1100	4.2	3.4	1.1	0.4
1200	1800	1700	2300				

Differences ROZELLE COVE

| -0038 | -0018 | -0036 | -0014 | +0.2 | -0.2 | +0.5 | +0.2 |

Port Fraser	0922 UT 3.8
	1527 UT 0.9

If HW Port Fraser is at 0000 or 1200, HW Rozelle Cove is 38 minutes earlier (-0038).
If HW Port Fraser is at 0600 or 1800, HW Rozelle Cove is 18 minutes earlier (-0018).
If LW Port Fraser is at 0500 or 1700, LW Rozelle Cove is 36 minutes earlier (-0036).
If LW Port Fraser is at 1100 or 2300, LW Rozelle Cove is 14 minutes earlier (-0014).

To make corrections when in between these times, you must interpolate. You can estimate the differences, but if you need more accuracy draw a graph.*

Example

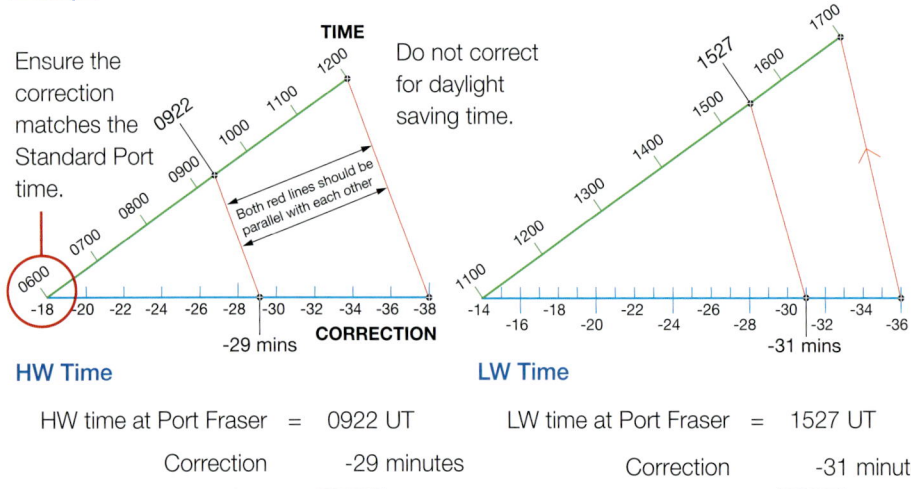

HW Time

HW time at Port Fraser	=	0922 UT
Correction		-29 minutes
HW time at Rozelle Cove	=	0853 UT
	=	0953 DST

LW Time

LW time at Port Fraser	=	1527 UT
Correction		-31 minutes
LW time at Rozelle Cove	=	1456 UT
	=	1556 DST

To find the height of tide between HW and LW put the secondary port HW height and times on the standard port curve.

*There are other ways to do this, such as mathematically, or using parallel lines as shown in DSN RYA Day Skipper Shorebased Notes.

SECONDARY PORT CALCULATIONS

A similar process can take place with heights.

Standard Port PORT FRASER (←)

Times				Height (metres)				
High Water		Low Water		MHWS	MHWN	MLWN	MLWS	
0000	0600	0500	1100	4.2	3.4	1.1	0.4	
1200	1800	1700	2300					
Differences ROZELLE COVE								
-0038	-0018	-0036	-0014	+0.2	-0.2	+0.5	+0.2	

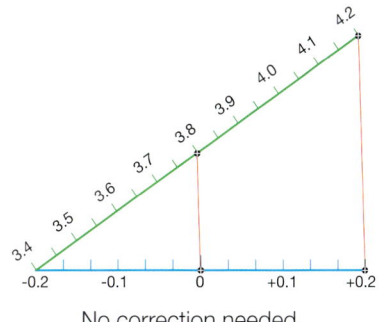

No correction needed.

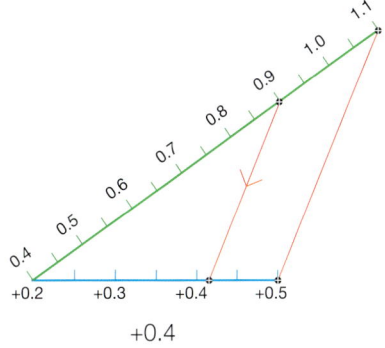

+0.4

HW Height

Rozelle Cove HW = 3.8m

LW Height

LW at Port Fraser	=	0.9
Correction	=	+0.4
LW at Rozelle Cove	=	1.3 m

THEREFORE
Rozelle Cove on Wednesday 24 April
HW 0953 DST 3.8m
LW 1556 DST 1.3m

This can be used on the Standard Port curve.

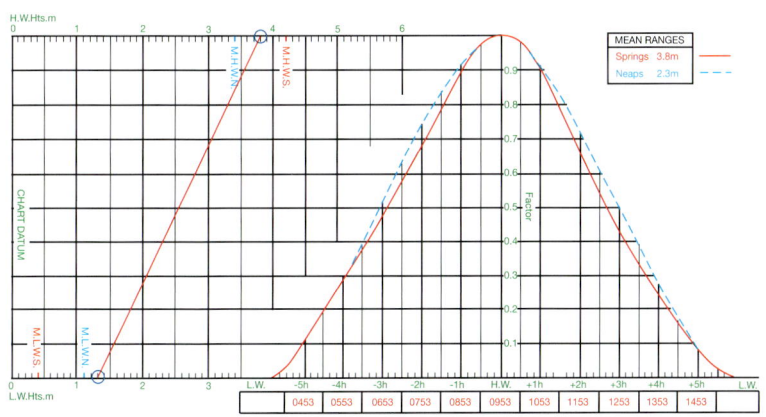

[23]

Tidal Streams

Consider the Tide as a Travelator

Go against the flow
= slow travel

Go with the flow =
quicker travel

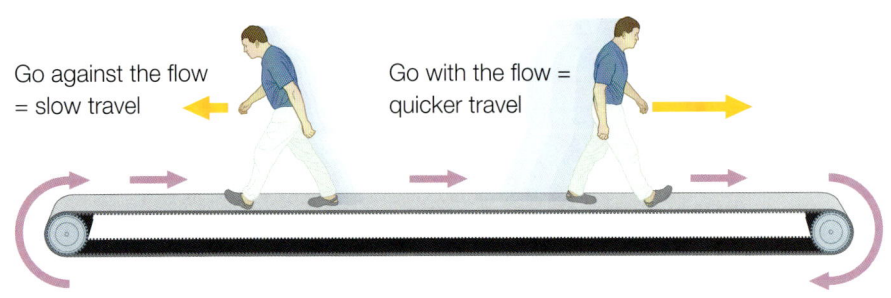

If you travel across the tidal stream the boat will be pushed sideways, giving a different ground track to the course you are steering.

The direction and rate of tidal streams depends on:
- Your location
- Whether it is springs, neaps or between the two
- The time relative to high water at a reference port.

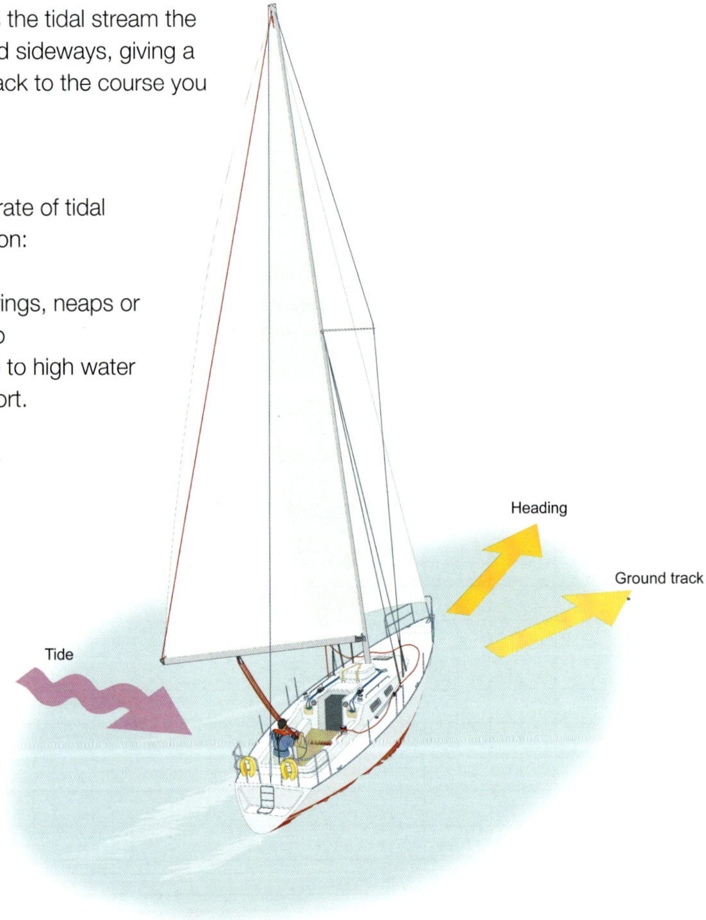

Heading

Ground track

Tide

Finding the Direction and Rate of the Tide

Tidal Stream Atlas

Tidal Diamond from Chart

Victoria A

Hours		A 46°20'5 N 5 50·0W	
Before High Water 6	−6	110	1·8 0·8
5	−5	108	1·0 0·5
4	−4	026	0·4 0·2
3	−3	297	1·4 0·7
2	−2	278	2·0 1·1
1	−1	274	1·7 0·8
High Water	0	271	1·1 0·5
After High Water 1	+1	170	0·5 0·3
2	+2	111	1·6 0·8
3	+3	114	1·8 0·9
4	+4	113	2·2 1·2
5	+5	112	2·0 1·0
6	+6	110	1·8 0·9

Spring rate (kn)

Neap rate (kn)

Direction (°T)

Time relative to HW of reference port

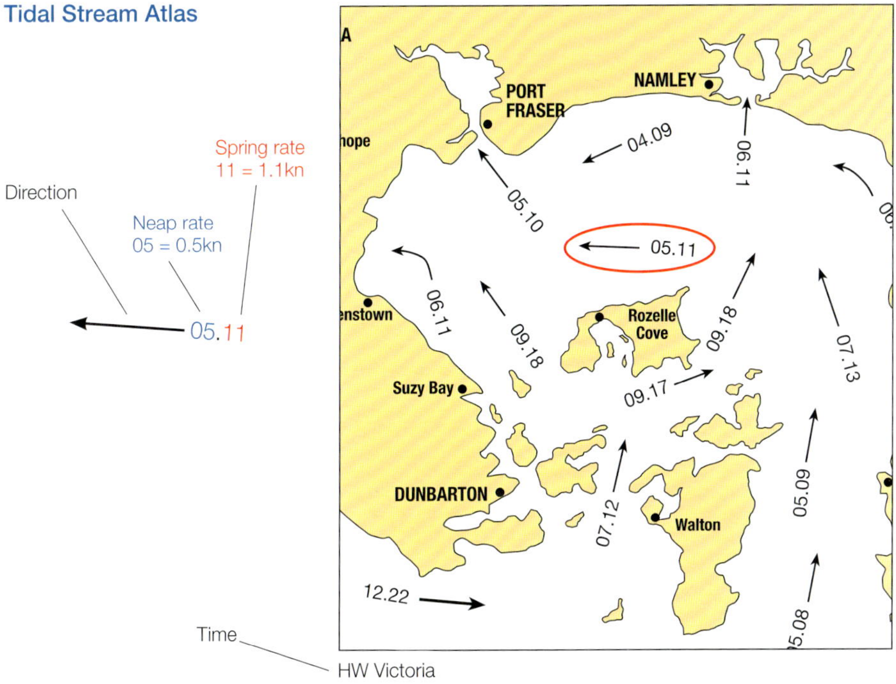

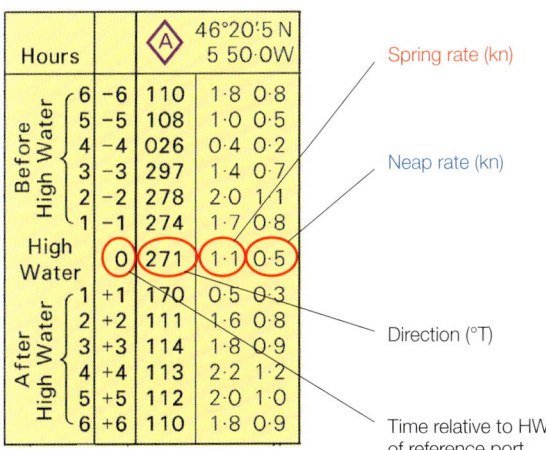

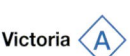

TIDAL STREAMS

Example

What is the direction and rate of the tidal stream 5 miles south-south-west of Namley Harbour on Monday 19th August at 1100 DST?

1 Find the time of HW and the heights of HW & LW at Victoria on Monday 19th August.

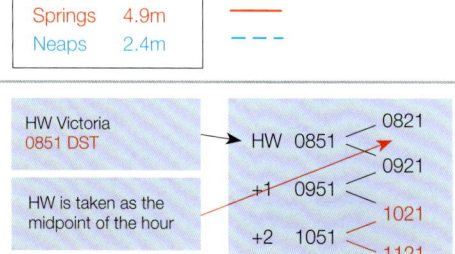

	Time	m
19	0123	1.7
	0751	4.7
M	1354	1.7
	2012	5.0

0751 UT
0851 DST is the nearest HW

2 Is it springs, neaps or in between?

```
        4.7
      - 1.7
Range  3.0m  = Mid Range
```

MEAN RANGES	
Springs	4.9m
Neaps	2.4m

3 How many hours before or after HW does 0900 fall?

HW Victoria
0851 DST

HW is taken as the midpoint of the hour

Answer +2 hours

HW 0851 — 0821, 0921
+1 0951 — 1021
+2 1051 — 1121

4 Find the nearest tidal diamond to your position = Ⓐ

Spring rate = 1.6kn   Neap rate = 0.8
Direction of tidal stream = 111°(T)

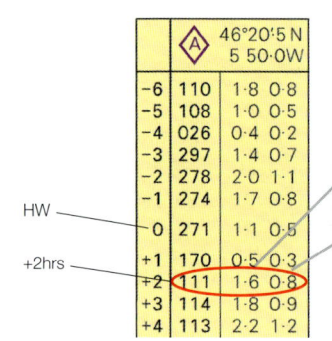

	Ⓐ 46°20'·5 N 5 50·0 W	
-6	110	1·8 0·8
-5	108	1·0 0·5
-4	026	0·4 0·2
-3	297	1·4 0·7
-2	278	2·0 1·1
-1	274	1·7 0·8
HW → 0	271	1·1 0·5
+1	170	0·5 0·3
+2hrs → +2	111	1·6 0·8
+3	114	1·8 0·9
+4	113	2·2 1·2

5 Or using a tidal stream atlas, which is the nearest arrow?

Measure direction of arrow 111°(T). Spring rate 1.6kn

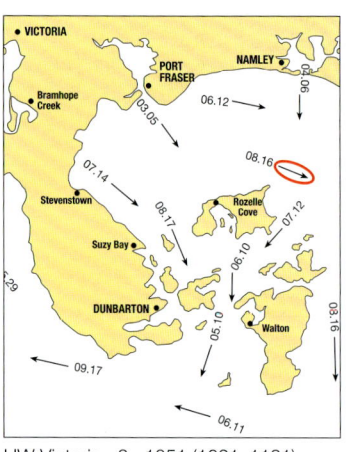

HW Victoria +2   1051 (1021–1121)

TIDAL STREAMS

Use a computation of rates table to find out the exact strength. N.B. This can also be done mathematically.

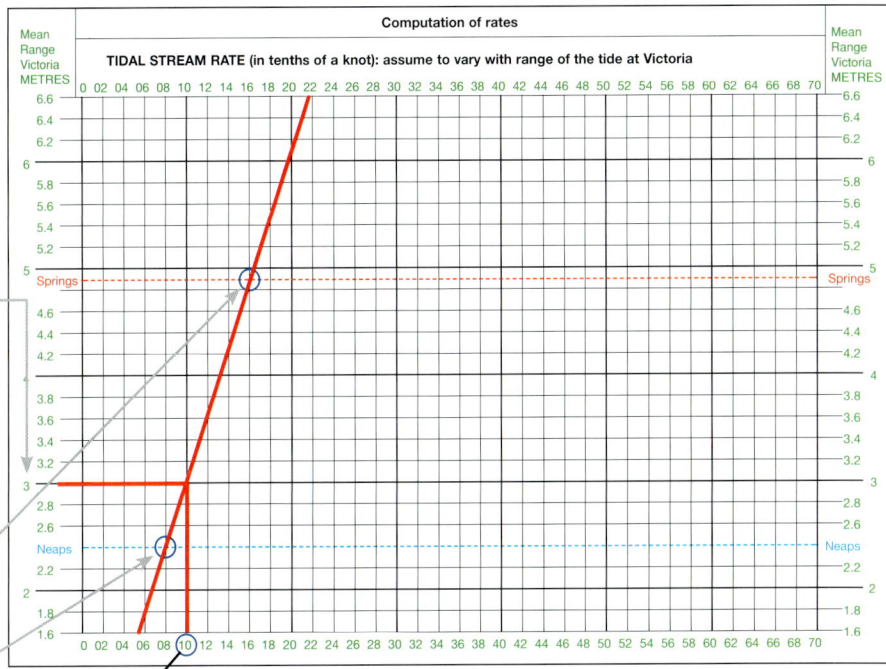

Rate = 1.0 knots

Instructions
1. From the tide tables, calculate the range of the tide for the day in question.
2. Note the neap and spring rate from the Tidal Stream Atlas or Tidal diamond for the required time and geographical position.
3. On this graph, plot the neap and spring rate on the relevant (neap or spring) dashed line, using the horizontal scale (Tidal Stream Rate).
4. Using a pencil and a straightedge, join the two plotted rates and extend the line to the extremities of the graph.
5. Using the calculated range from step 1, enter the vertical (Mean Range) scale. Draw a horizontal line to intercept the pencil line drawn in step 4.
6. At this interception, draw a line vertically, up or down, and read off on the horizontal scale the rate of the tidal stream for the calculated range.

Tidal data is also available through apps or websites.

Tidal Overfalls, Races & Eddies

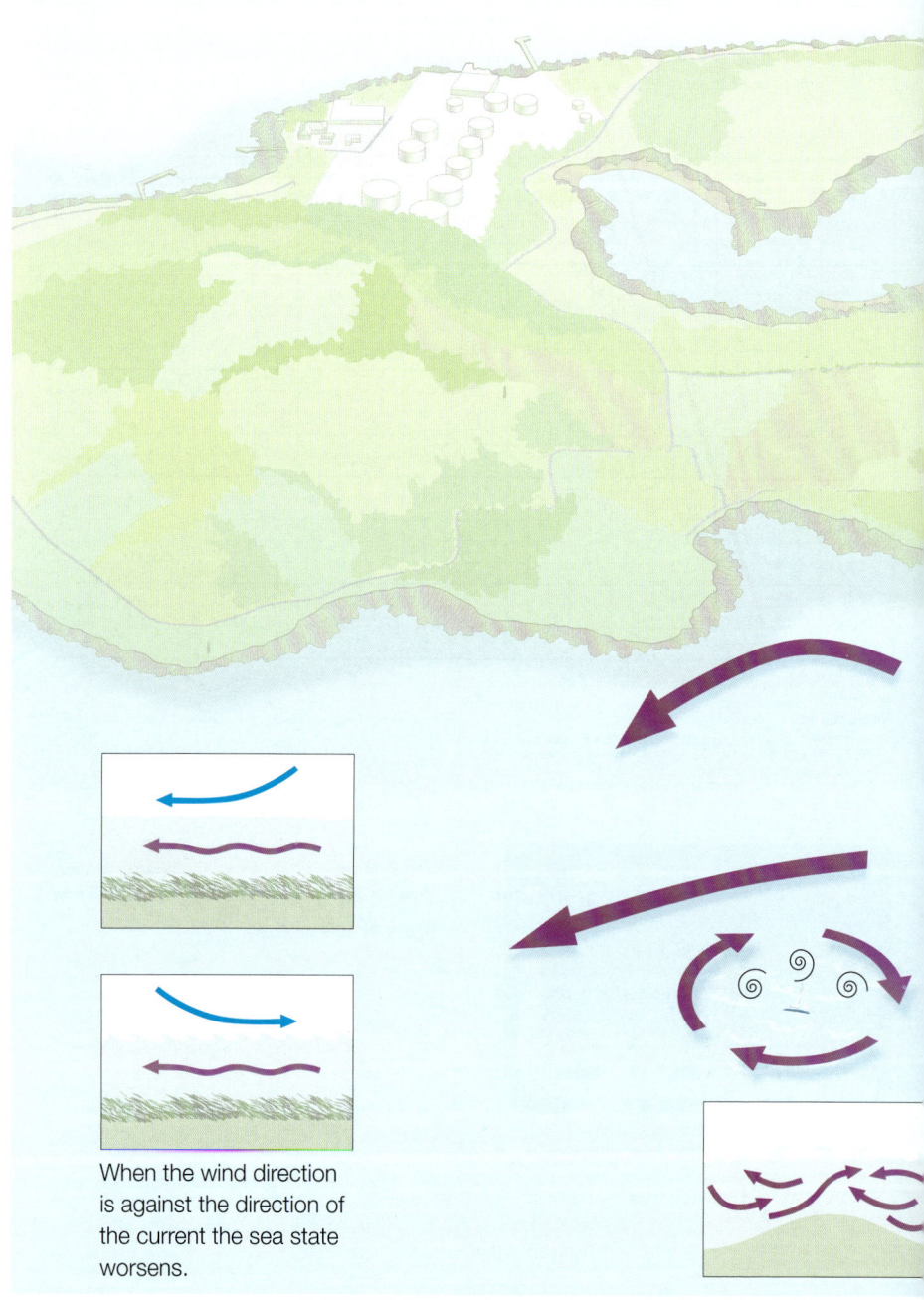

When the wind direction is against the direction of the current the sea state worsens.

TIDAL OVERFALLS, RACES & EDDIES

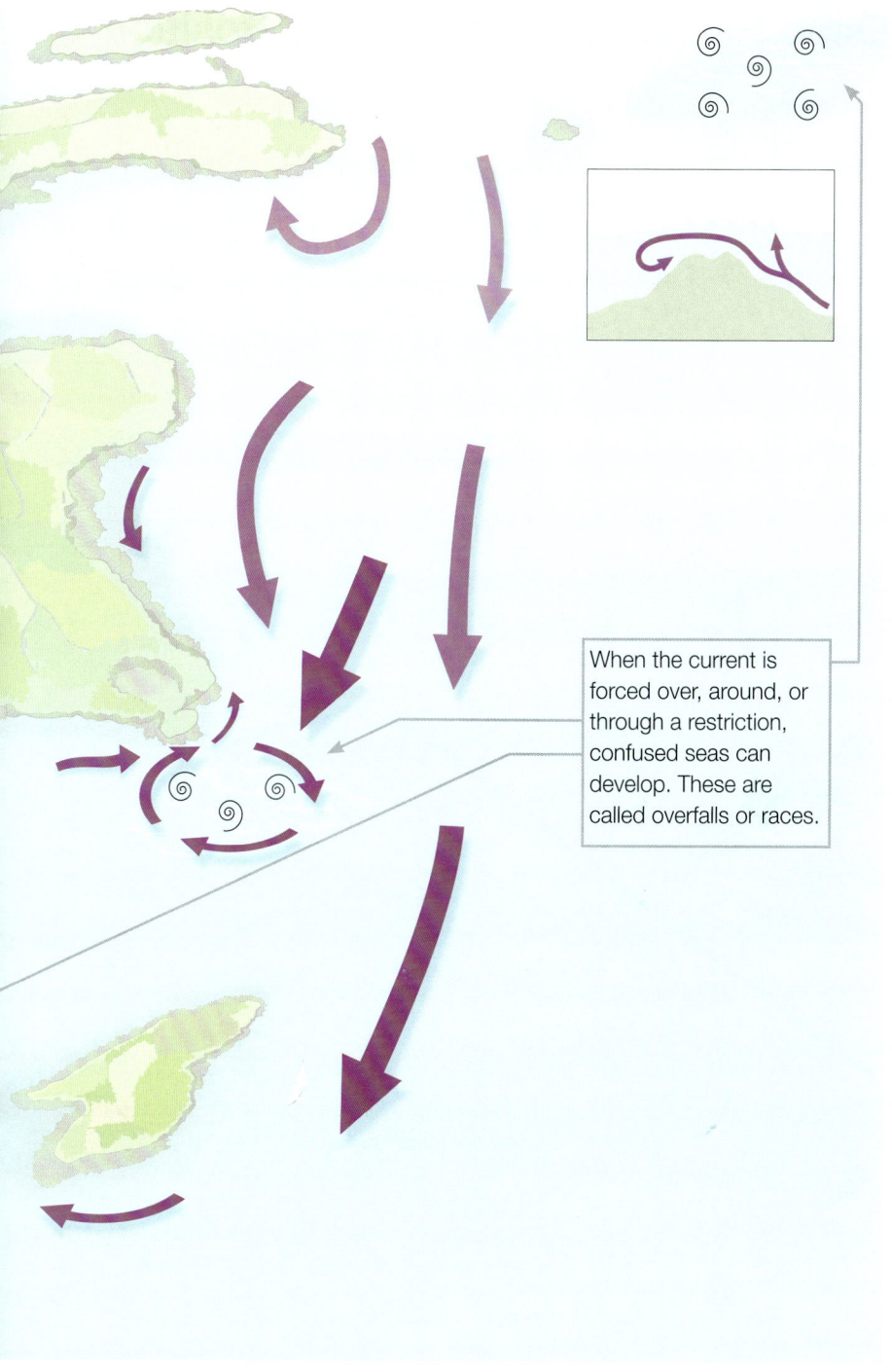

When the current is forced over, around, or through a restriction, confused seas can develop. These are called overfalls or races.

Dead Reckoning & Estimated Position

It is possible to reckon your approximate position if you know:
- the course steered
- the distance travelled (measured by log).

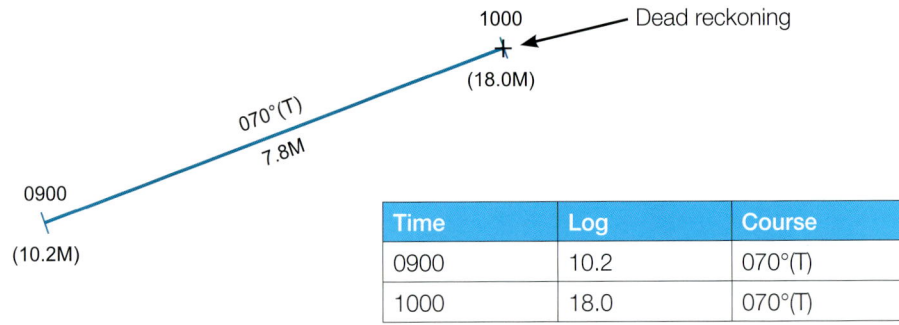

Time	Log	Course
0900	10.2	070°(T)
1000	18.0	070°(T)

(7.8 miles travelled)

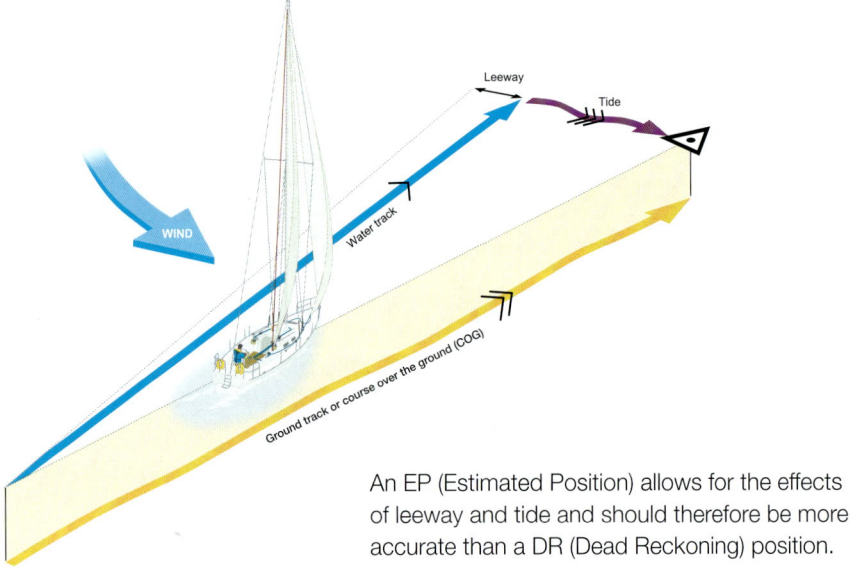

An EP (Estimated Position) allows for the effects of leeway and tide and should therefore be more accurate than a DR (Dead Reckoning) position.

Leeway – If the wind is on your port side, add leeway before you plot the water track. If the wind is on your starboard side, subtract leeway.

DEAD RECKONING & ESTIMATED POSITION

To Plot an EP

Time	Log	Course	Leeway	Wind	Tide
0900	10.2	070°(T)	5°	N6	140°(T) 1.4kn
1000	18.0	070°(T)	5°	N6	120°(T) 2.0kn tide for 0900–1000

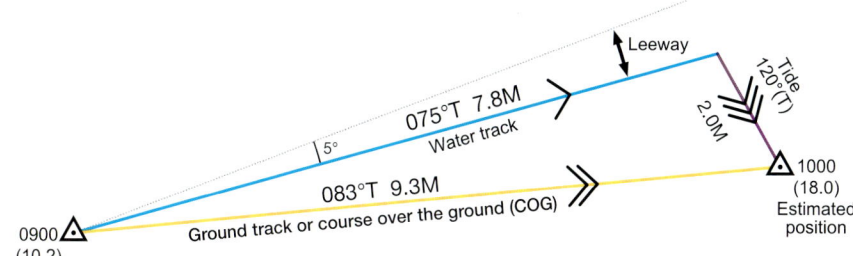

Projected EP

If you can predict your boatspeed and how the tide will affect you, it's possible to work out a projected EP (an EP in advance). This is very useful for calculating your future ground track. "Will I hit the rocks on this heading?" Yes.

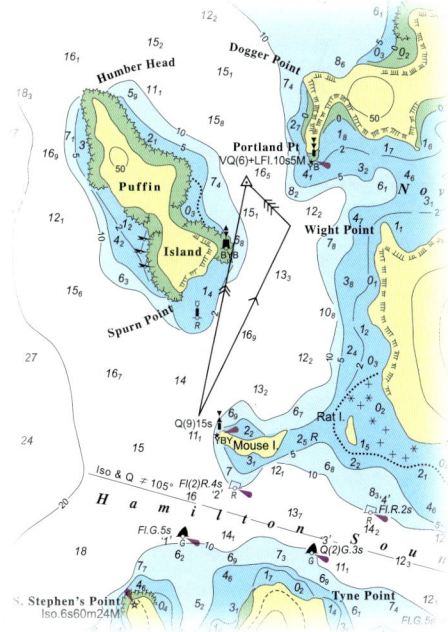

[31]

DEAD RECKONING & ESTIMATED POSITION

The accuracy of an EP depends on:

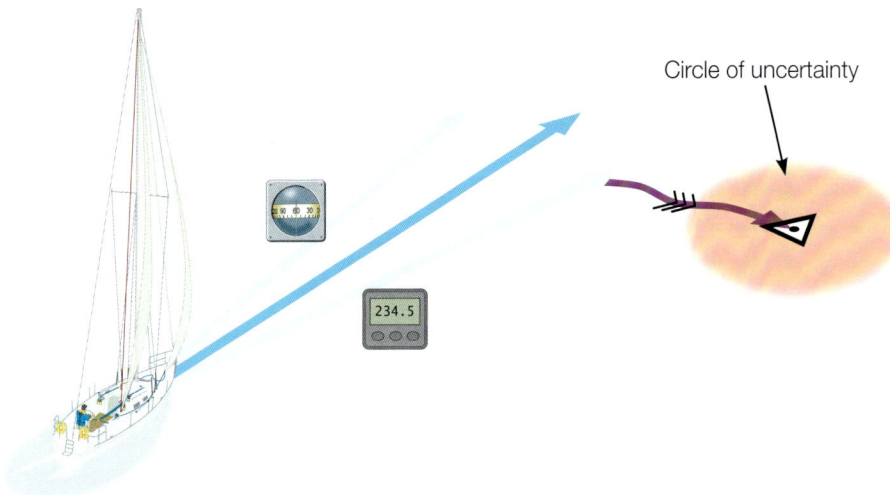

Circle of uncertainty

These factors combined mean that it's unlikely you are at the exact position on the chart where you have plotted your EP. You can allow for this by assuming that your position is within a circle of uncertainty, which in rough weather and strong tides can be about 10 per cent of the distance travelled.

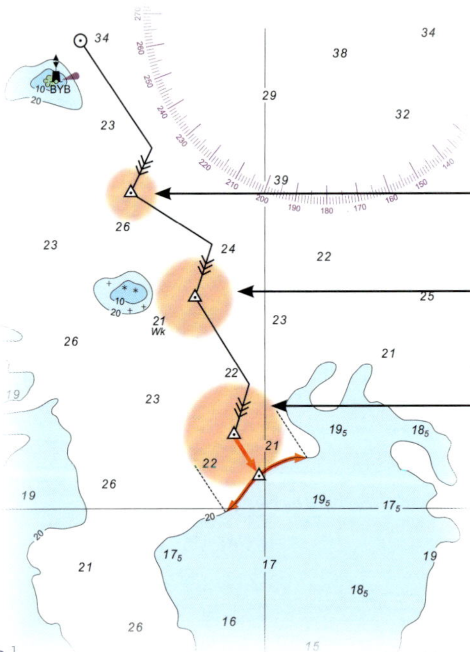

As you proceed further into your passage the circle will grow larger.

Navigate to keep hazards outside the circle.

You can reduce this circle if you have more information, e.g. as you cross the 20m contour the circle becomes a line of uncertainty.

Fixing your Position

Using Visual Bearings

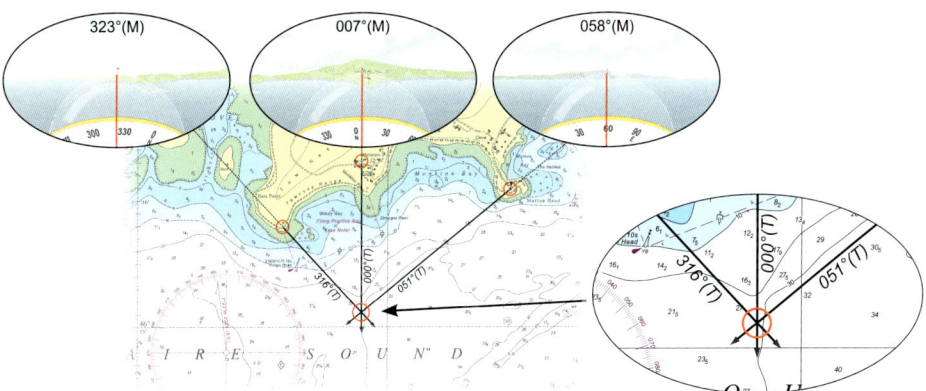

If you can readily relate symbols on the chart with features you can see, you can fix your position by taking a bearing of each feature with a hand bearing compass. When you plot these bearings on the chart you can fix your position where the bearings intersect.

In reality, you are unlikely to get a very precise fix. Compass error and your distance from the feature mean you will have a cocked hat.

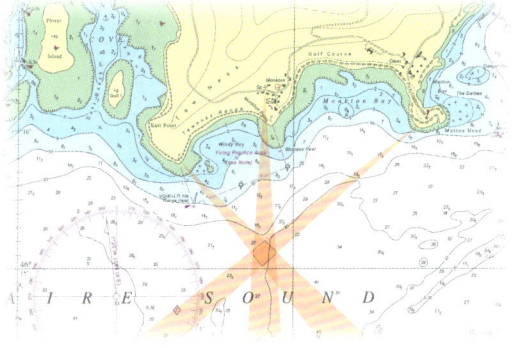

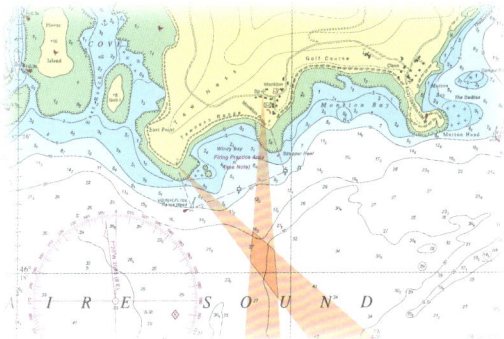

If you choose features which are too close together or at 180 degrees to each other your angle of cut will be poor, giving a less accurate position.

FIXING YOUR POSITION

When you are Moving

Bearing ❶ will change the least. Take this first.

Take bearing ❷ next.

Bearing ❸ will change the most. Take this last and record time and log. Best practice is to plot the last bearing first.

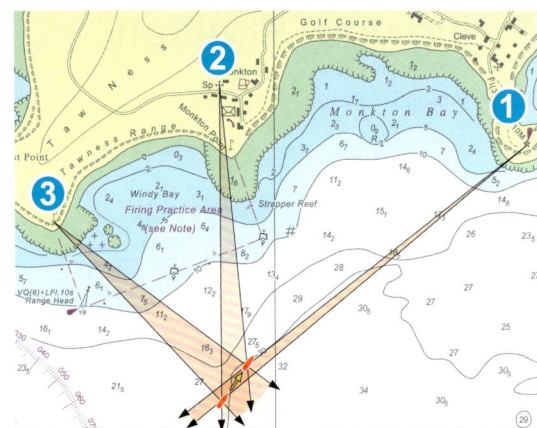

Accuracy

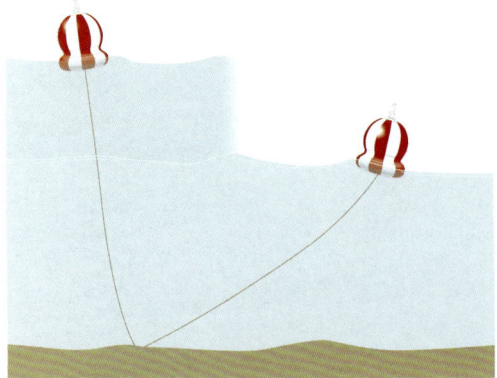

Take care when using buoys for a fix. They can move off station in bad weather and their position may change slightly as the tide rises and falls.

Use other sources of information to help you obtain a more accurate position. When using depth, remember to correct for the height of tide.

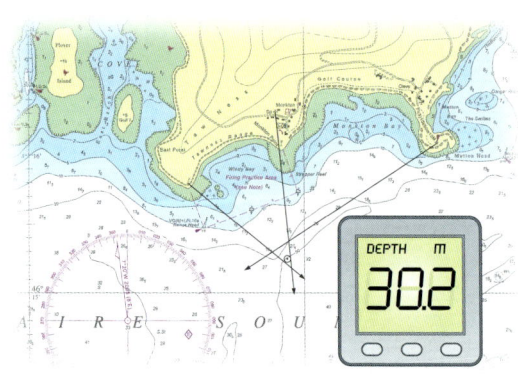

FIXING YOUR POSITION

	Position Line	Comments
Most accurate ↑	Charted Transit	Very accurate assuming correctly identified. Worth checking with a bearing.
	Radar Range	Accurate – errors tend to be due to human or system errors.
	Compass Bearing	
	Depth Contour	Inaccuracies possibly through tidal height errors, or with flat seabeds, old surveys, or inaccurate charts.
Least accurate ↓	Rising/Dipping Distance	Relies on correct depth & height calculation. More relevant on landfalls at night.

Simplest Fix
This can be taken when passing a charted object.

Transit and Contour
Always allow for the height of tide.

Transit and Bearing
If you use a bearing at about 90 degrees to a transit you will obtain the best angle of cut.

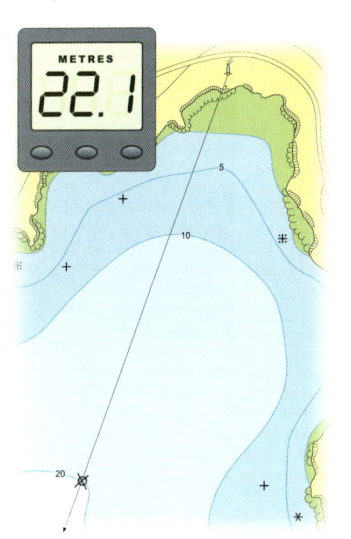

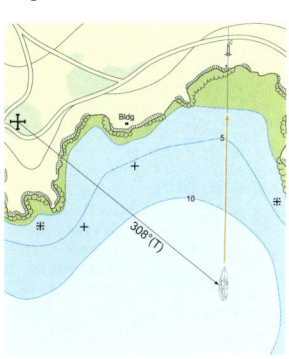

FIXING YOUR POSITION

Sector Light
Take a fix if you cross between sectors.

Radar Ranges
Radar can measure range very accurately. Use two or three ranges to obtain a fix. Whenever a position is established, note the time and log reading.

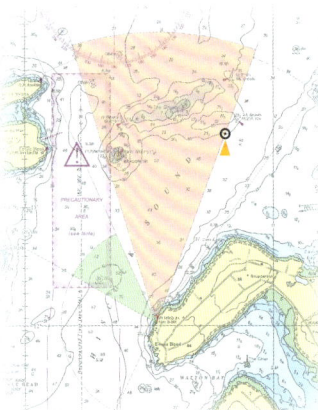

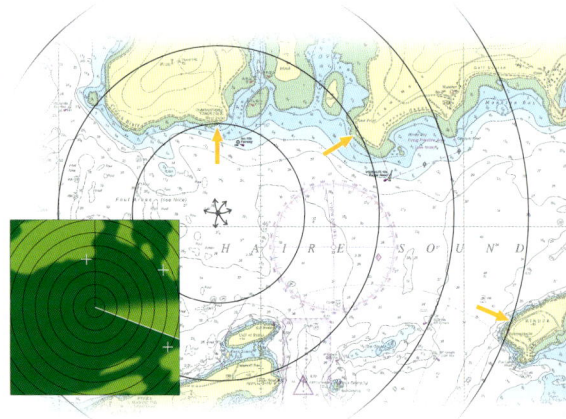

Radar Bearings
Use with caution as the average radar beam width is 5 degrees or more. The image on the display will seem stretched because of this, making measurement of an exact bearing difficult.

[36]

FIXING YOUR POSITION

Rising/Dipping Distance
Use tables from an almanac to give you the range from a lighthouse.

Running Fix
Two bearings taken at different times combined with an EP can give a fix.

First, take a bearing from a known object and plot that line (a). After running for a known distance, take a second bearing from the same object and plot this on the chart. Plot your boat's water track (a to b) at any point along the first visual fix. Then plot your boat's tidal set and drift (b to c). Then, using your parallel rule, draw a line parallel to your first visual fix line (the transferred position line).

Transferred position line
This line is made parallel to the first visual fix line, starting from the end of the tidal drift at (c) and intersecting the second visual fix line at (d) to give you an estimated position

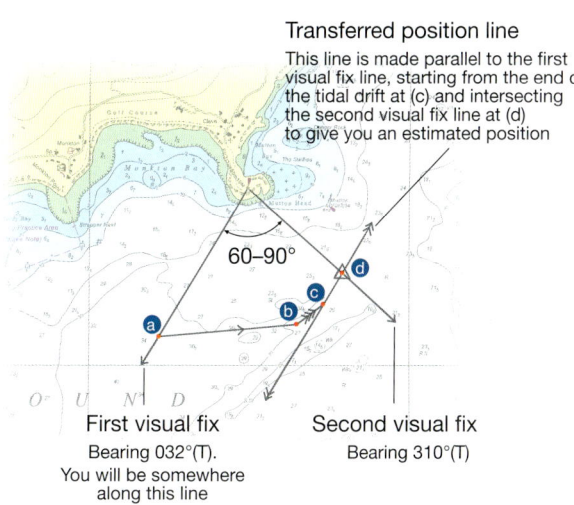

First visual fix
Bearing 032°(T).
You will be somewhere along this line

Second visual fix
Bearing 310°(T)

Plotting Symbols

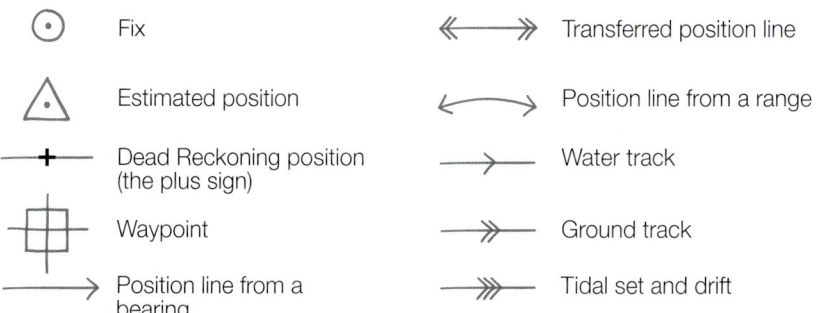

⊙	Fix	⇔	Transferred position line
△	Estimated position	⟷	Position line from a range
+	Dead Reckoning position (the plus sign)	→	Water track
⊞	Waypoint	⇉	Ground track
→	Position line from a bearing	⇶	Tidal set and drift

Global Navigation Satellite Systems (GNSS)

There are two prominent GNSSs – the American Global Positioning System (GPS) and the Russian Globalnaya Navigazionnaya Sputnikovaya Sistema (GLONASS). They both work in the same way and many receivers can use both.

GNSS Position Fixing
A GNSS receiver obtains a fix from signals transmitted from orbiting satellites.

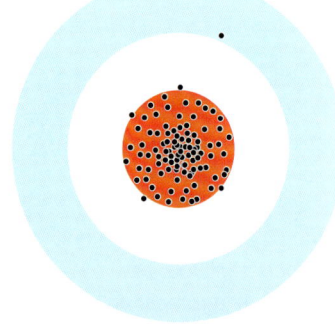

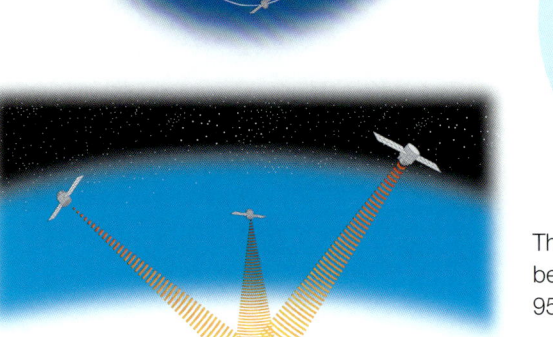

This gives a position which can be accurate to within 15 metres 95 per cent of the time.

Site your aerial low down to avoid signal bounce and thus a less-accurate position fix. Ensure it has a clear view of the entire sky and is not shielded in any way.

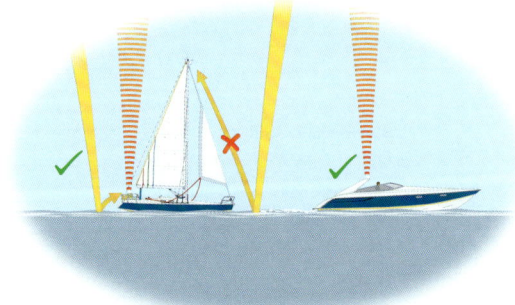

GLOBAL NAVIGATION SATELLITE SYSTEMS (GNSS)

HDoP (Horizontal Dilution of Precision)

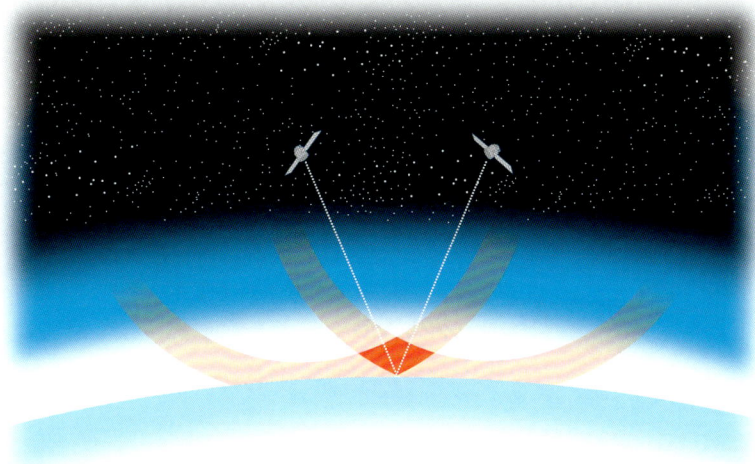

Low HDoP.
Theoretical best = Value of 1.4
Double figures = Poor accuracy
Low HDoP = Good

High HDoP.
High HDoP reduces the precision of the fix due to a poor cut from the satellite signals, similar to the error when bearings are taken from objects which are too close together.

GLOBAL NAVIGATION SATELLITE SYSTEMS (GNSS)

Back up
Always back up your GNSS position with information from another source.

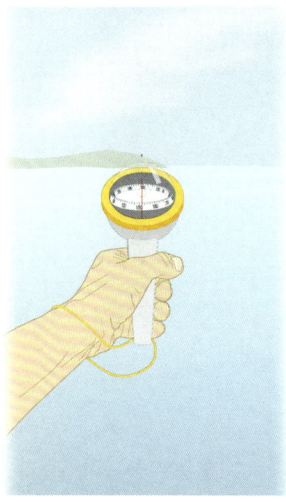

Bearing.

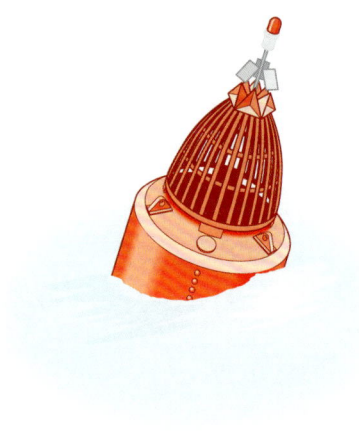

A charted object (IALA B buoyage).

Radar range/bearing.

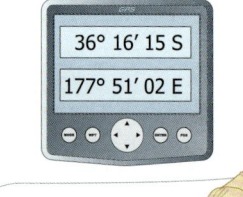

Keep a record of your position at regular intervals on the chart and in the ship's log.

Depth allowing for height of tide; distance to run.

GLOBAL NAVIGATION SATELLITE SYSTEMS (GNSS)

GNSS – Good Practice

Retrospective plotting of your GNSS position means you will always be playing catch-up. Pilotage is often a more appropriate method of navigation when you are navigating in close proximity to any hazards.

Reliability

GNSS is generally reliable and accurate but as with all electronics it can go wrong. Common things to watch out for are:

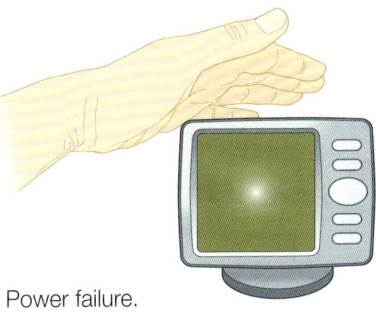

Power failure.

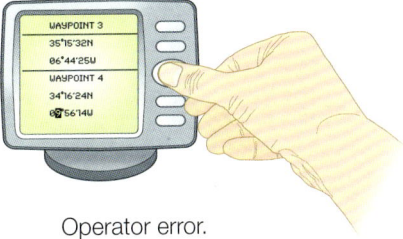

Operator error.

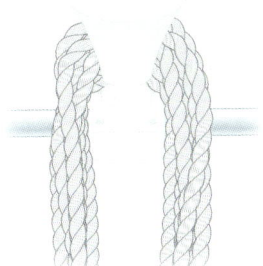

Poorly sited or shielded aerial.

Interruption or changes to the satellite system.

GLOBAL NAVIGATION SATELLITE SYSTEMS (GNSS)

GNSS Set-up and Display

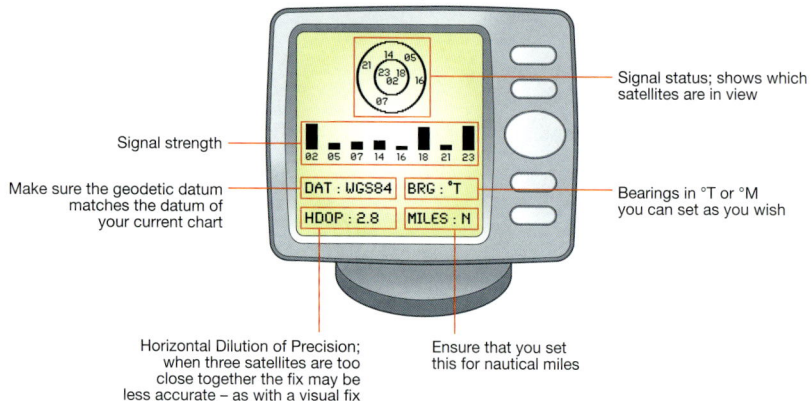

Signal status; shows which satellites are in view

Signal strength

Make sure the geodetic datum matches the datum of your current chart

Bearings in °T or °M you can set as you wish

Horizontal Dilution of Precision; when three satellites are too close together the fix may be less accurate – as with a visual fix

Ensure that you set this for nautical miles

GNSS Waypoints

Waypoints are tools to help you navigate. They are positions stored in the memory of a GNSS and used as reference points.

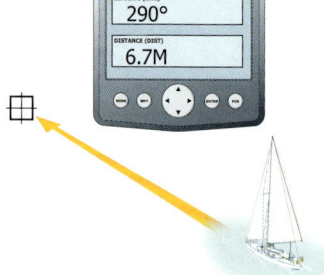

You can obtain waypoints from publications such as almanacs, directories, and magazines.

Cross-track Error

This function shows your lateral distance from the rhumb line between two waypoints.

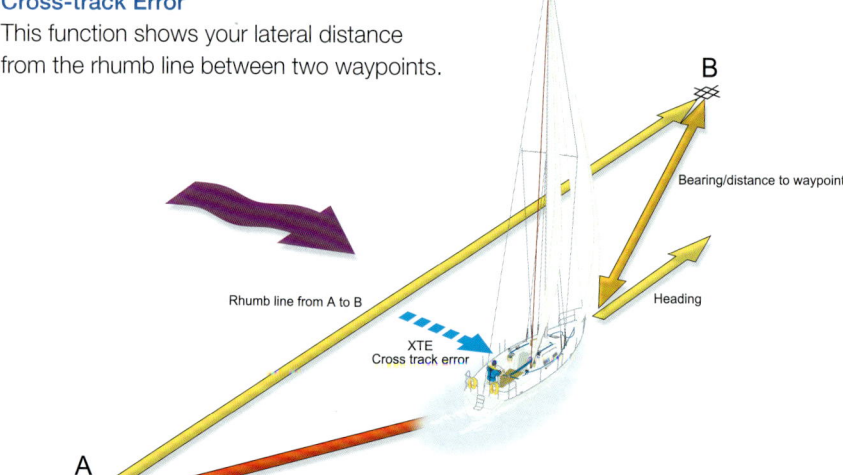

Bearing/distance to waypoint

Heading

XTE Cross track error

Rhumb line from A to B

Course and speed over the ground

GLOBAL NAVIGATION SATELLITE SYSTEMS (GNSS)

GNSS – Other Functions

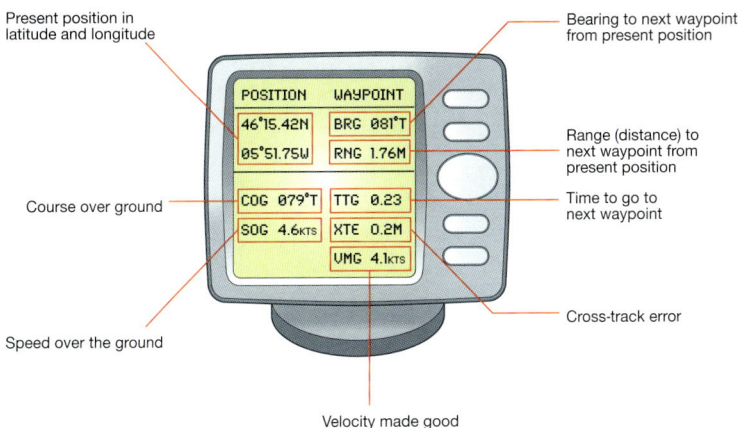

- Present position in latitude and longitude
- Course over ground
- Speed over the ground
- Bearing to next waypoint from present position
- Range (distance) to next waypoint from present position
- Time to go to next waypoint
- Cross-track error
- Velocity made good

Velocity Made Good

The velocity made good function displays your progress towards a waypoint. Here, port tack has a higher velocity made good than starboard.

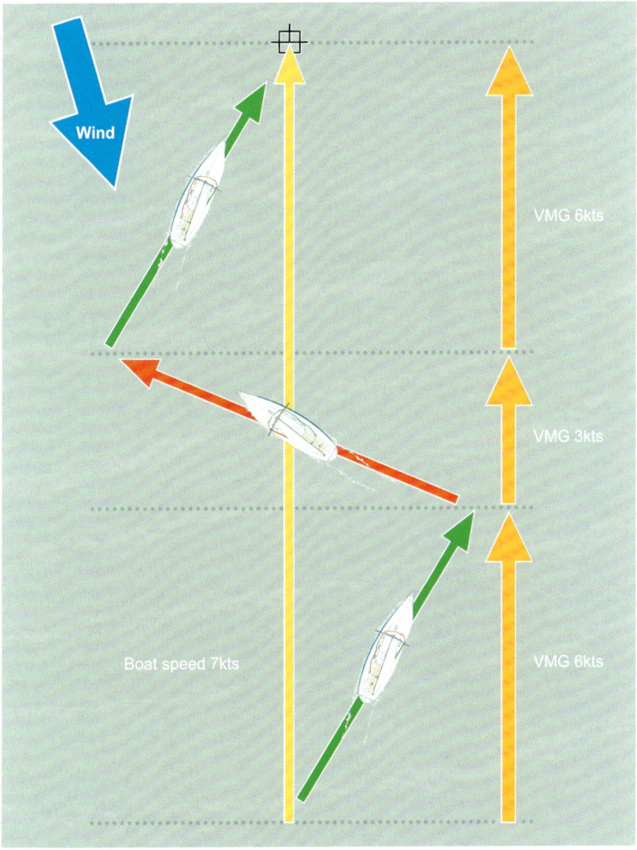

[43]

GLOBAL NAVIGATION SATELLITE SYSTEMS (GNSS)

Using GNSS – Routes

You can enter a series of waypoints into a GNSS to make a route. Again, always plot the waypoints on the chart and double-check the distances and bearings between each.

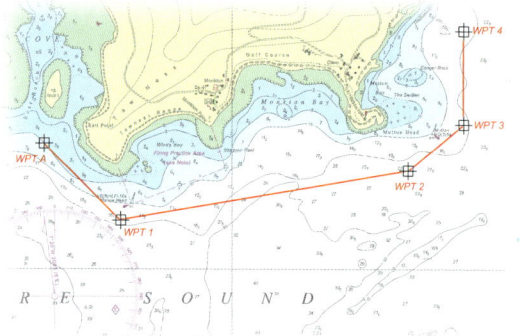

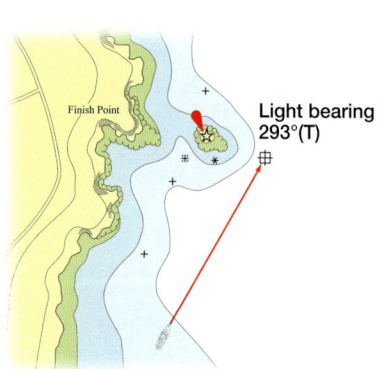

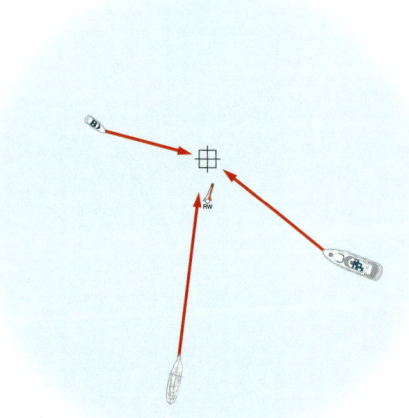

Plot your waypoint adjacent to rather than directly on charted objects. You could hit them!

In busy areas, bear in mind that lots of boats could be using the same waypoint.

[44]

GLOBAL NAVIGATION SATELLITE SYSTEMS (GNSS)

Remember that GNSS doesn't allow for tidal stream.

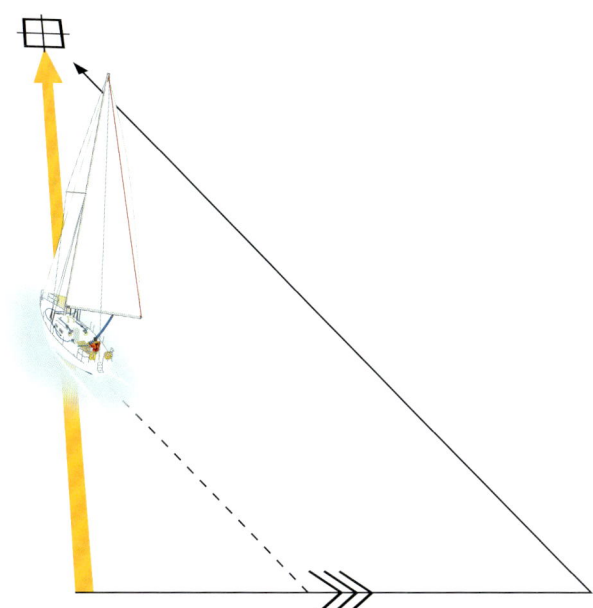

Always pre-plan a course to steer to allow for tidal stream. It's more efficient.

It seems easy just to steer the direction to a waypoint that the GNSS gives, but if there is significant crosstide you will sail a longer route and could put the boat in danger.

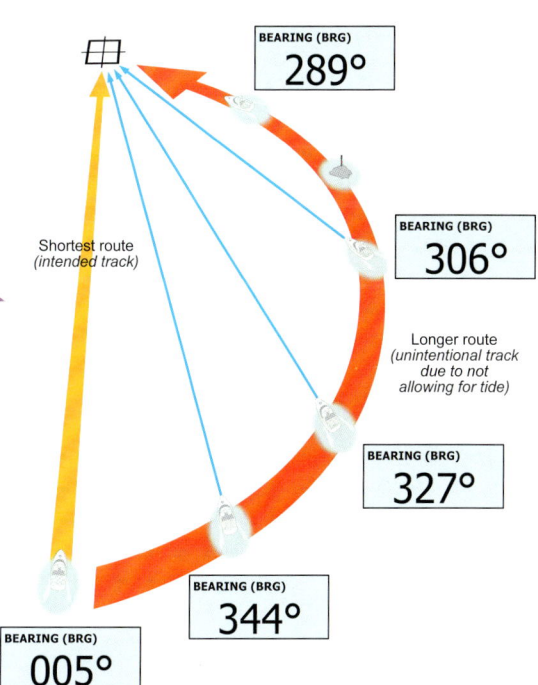

Using Text-based GNSS Receivers with Paper Charts

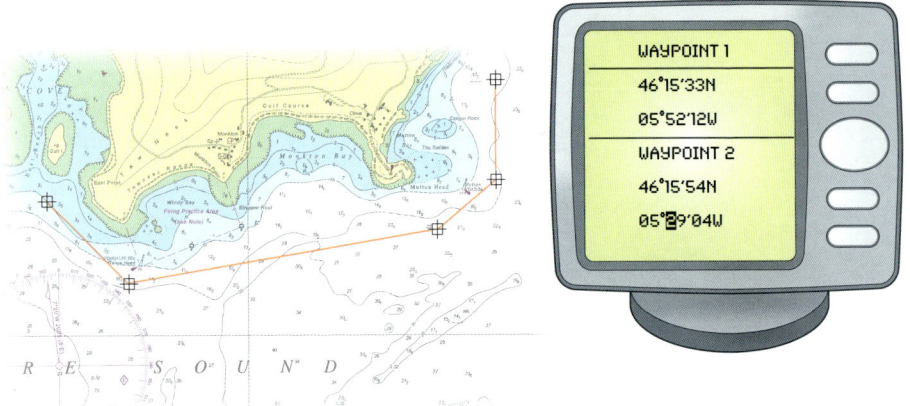

Take care when putting waypoint positions into a GNSS receiver. It's as easy to miskey latitude and longitude as it is to dial a wrong phone number.

USING TEXT-BASED GNSS RECEIVERS WITH PAPER CHARTS

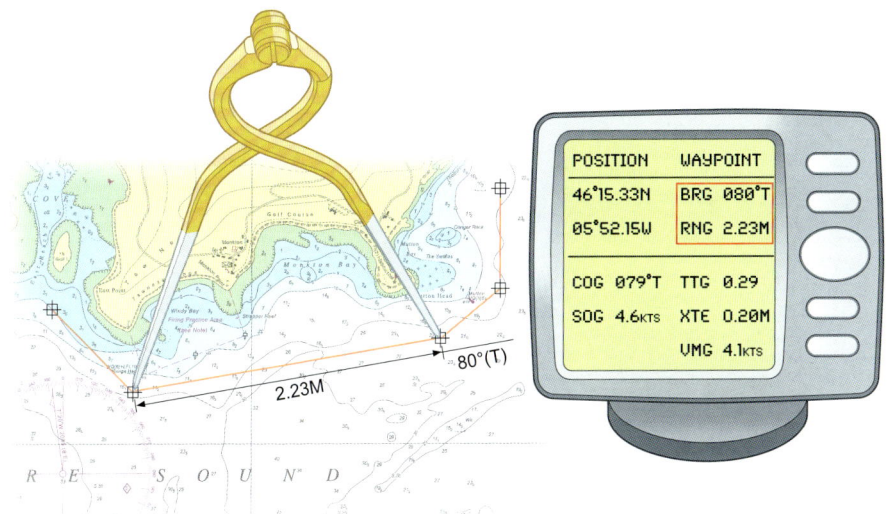

Before relying on GNSS information such as the distance and bearing to a waypoint, check that it's correct by plotting it on a chart.

USING TEXT-BASED GNSS RECEIVERS WITH PAPER CHARTS

Using a Compass Rose

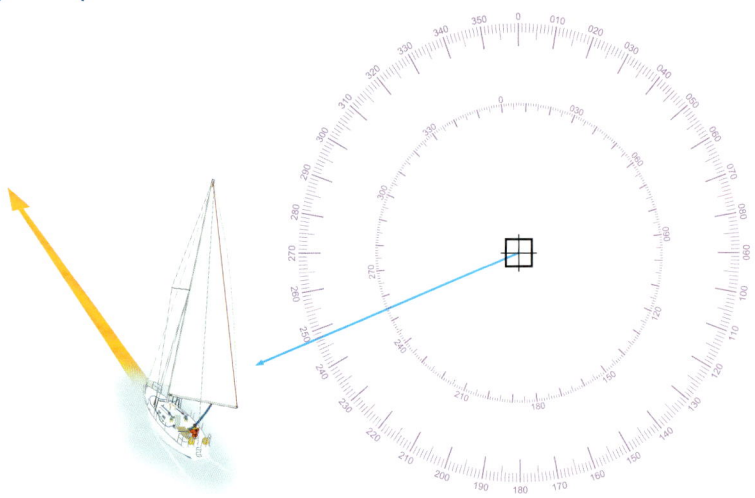

You can plot your position quickly and simply by entering easily found positions as waypoints. Your GNSS will give you a distance and bearing to a waypoint which you can plot on the chart as a fix. This is easier, quicker and less prone to error than plotting latitude and longitude, but double check that you have entered the waypoint correctly.

Plotting at Speed

Conventional plotting can be difficult on a fast boat at speed. Navigation must be pre-planned.

USING TEXT-BASED GNSS RECEIVERS WITH PAPER CHARTS

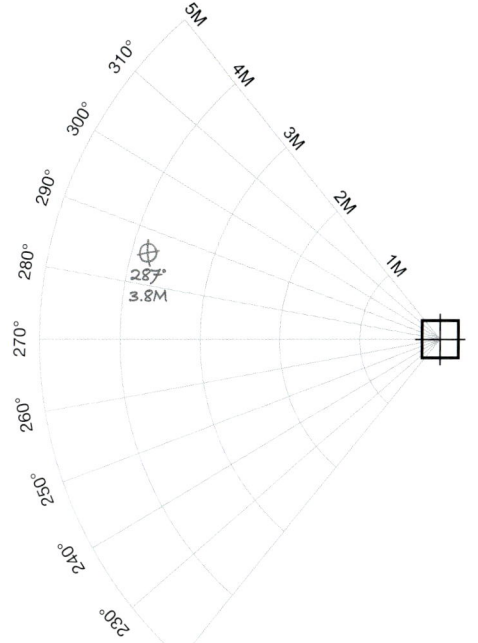

Pre-draw a web of distances and bearings from your waypoint. Compare the distance and bearing to the waypoint within the web to find your position.

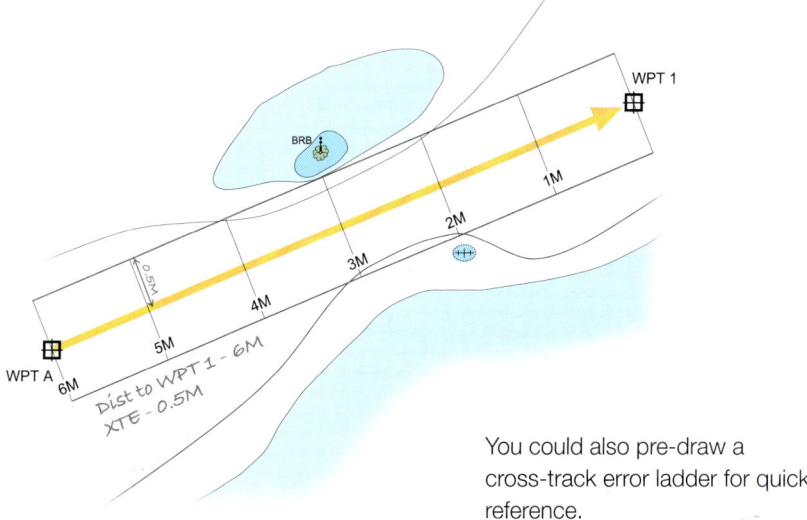

You could also pre-draw a cross-track error ladder for quick reference.

[49]

Electronic Charts & Chart Plotters

The Two Main Types
There are two styles of electronic charts: raster and vector.

Raster charts are exact electronic copies of paper charts, so they are instantly familiar to those used to them.

Vector charts are constructed from a database of positons and features, which allows the chart to be modified to hide or show certain 'layers' of information, e.g. spot depths. Vector charts automatically adjust the amount of detail shown as you zoom in and out of the chart. The symbols used on vector charts differ slightly to those used on paper charts.

Hydrographic offices produce official electronic charts just as they do paper charts. These are called Raster Navigation Charts (RNC) for raster charts, or Electronic Navigation Charts (ENC) for vector charts.

Only official electronic charts that meet international standards can be referred to as ENC or RNC. All others are referred to simply as electronic charts (EC), which are typically vector-based charts. Most leisure chart plotters use ECs and as a consequence display the warning 'Not to be used for navigation' in their start-up screens.

When determining how much to rely upon an electronic chart plotter as a primary navigational aid, assess the following:

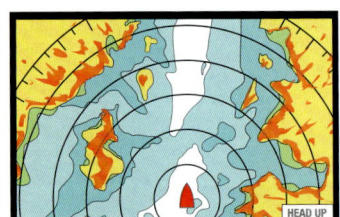

The chart:
- How reliable is the chart? Is it an ENC, RNC or EC?
- Can I verify whether the chart is up to date?

The GNSS fix:
- Can I verify the HDoP and quality of the fix?
- Can I plot a position independently of a GNSS fix?

If you cannot positively answer all of the above, the plotter in question is at best useful for situational awareness or rough planning.

The harsh marine environment and electronics don't always mix well.
- You should carry paper charts with a suitable coverage and an almanac.
- Be aware that your displayed position is from a single source.
- Always back it up with another source of information.
- Keep a separate record of your position.

Electronic Equipment

Depth Sounder

A depth sounder transmits ultrasonic signals which are reflected from the sea bed. Can be less accurate over soft mud and when going astern due to wash from the propeller.

Log

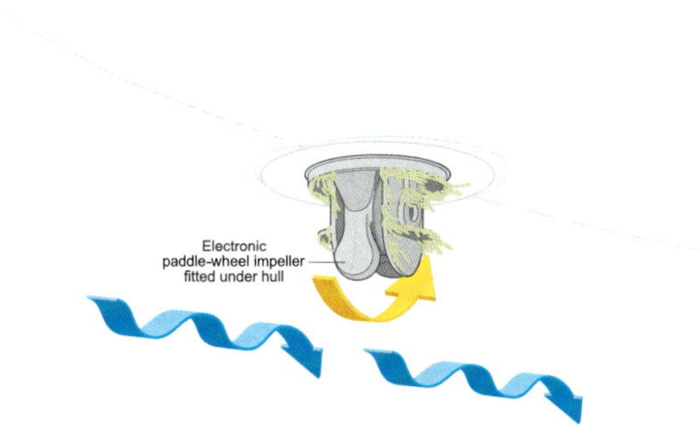

Fouling from weeds and barnacles affects accuracy. Clear regularly.

ELECTRONIC EQUIPMENT

Radar

An extremely versatile piece of equipment. Can be used for:

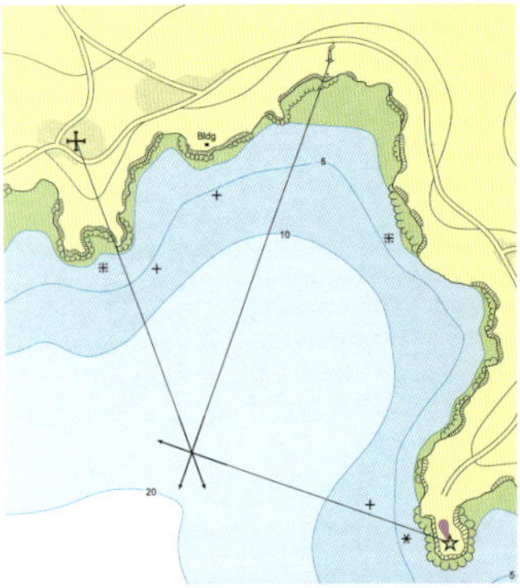

Navigation.

Detecting objects in the dark or poor visibility.

Collision avoidance. Steady relative bearing means you are on a collision course.

Course to Steer

A person rowing across a river instinctively angles the boat upstream to counter the effect of the current.

At sea we often can't see our destination so we need to calculate how much to angle into the tidal stream to make the most direct passage.

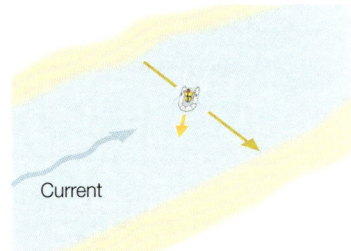
Current

For example:
What is the course to steer from position A to waypoint B at 1045 DST on Friday 24 May?

1 How far is it from A to B?
Answer: 8.5 miles.

2 Approximately how long will it take to travel 8.5 miles if my speed is 9 knots?
Answer: Roughly an hour.

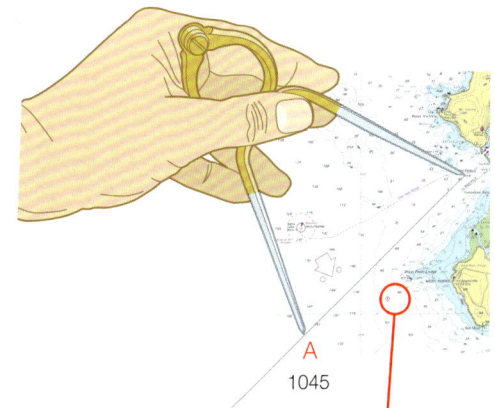
A
1045

3 Leaving position A at 1045, how will the tidal stream affect my passage for the next hour?

- Using RYA Training Chart 3, find the tidal stream reference port (Victoria).

- Find the time of HW and establish springs or neaps. Friday 24 May HW Victoria = 0916 DST range 4.9 (springs).

- Use the closest tidal diamond ⟨B⟩ to establish rate and direction. You could also use a tidal atlas.

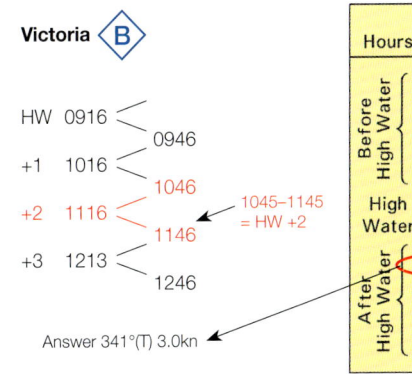

Victoria ⟨B⟩

HW 0916
        0946
+1 1016
        1046
+2 1116   1045–1145
        1146   = HW +2
+3 1213
        1246

Answer 341°(T) 3.0kn

	Hours	⟨B⟩	46°20'6 N 6 18·4 W
Before High Water	6	158	1·0 0·6
	5	153	1·7 0·8
	4	159	2·8 1·5
	3	154	3·9 2·0
	2	165	3·2 1·7
	1	173	2·4 1·3
High Water		186	1·2 0·7
After High Water	1	349	1·1 0·6
	2	341	3·0 1·6
	3	338	3·7 1·8
	4	342	3·9 2·0
	5	341	2·8 1·5
	6	355	2·3 1·2

[53]

COURSE TO STEER

4 Plot the tidal stream at the start of the ground track.

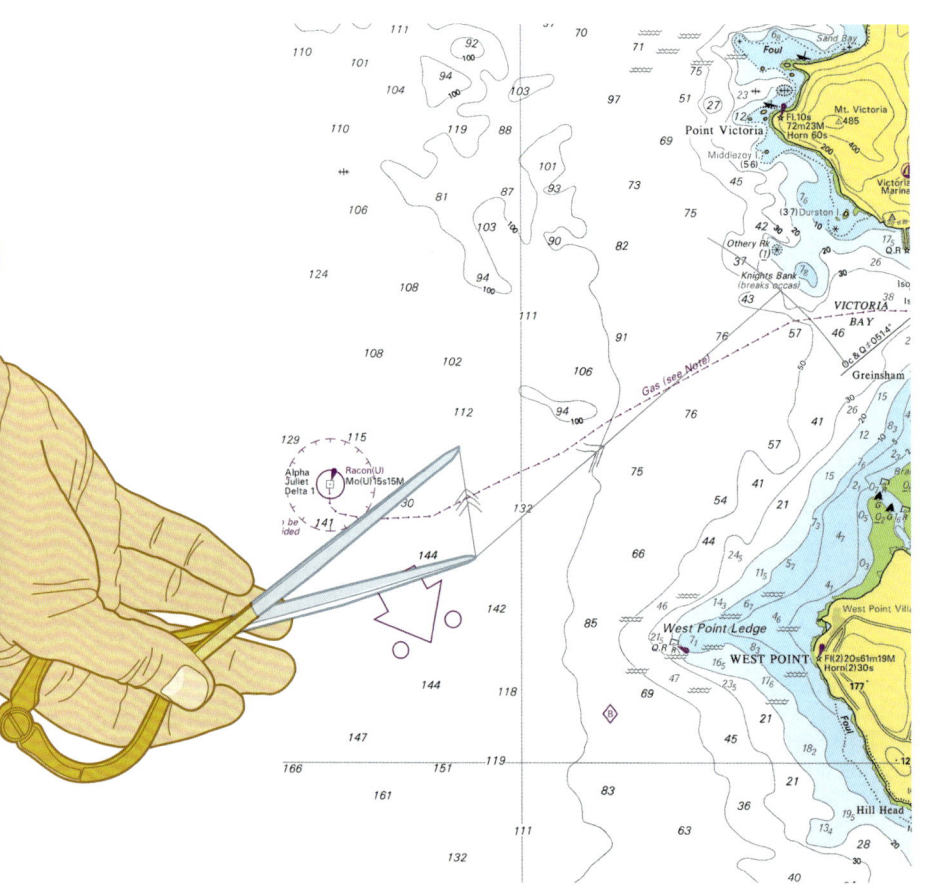

COURSE TO STEER

5 Measure the expected boat speed for one hour (9kn) and arc dividers from the end of the tidal stream to cross the ground track. This usually goes beyond or falls short of B.

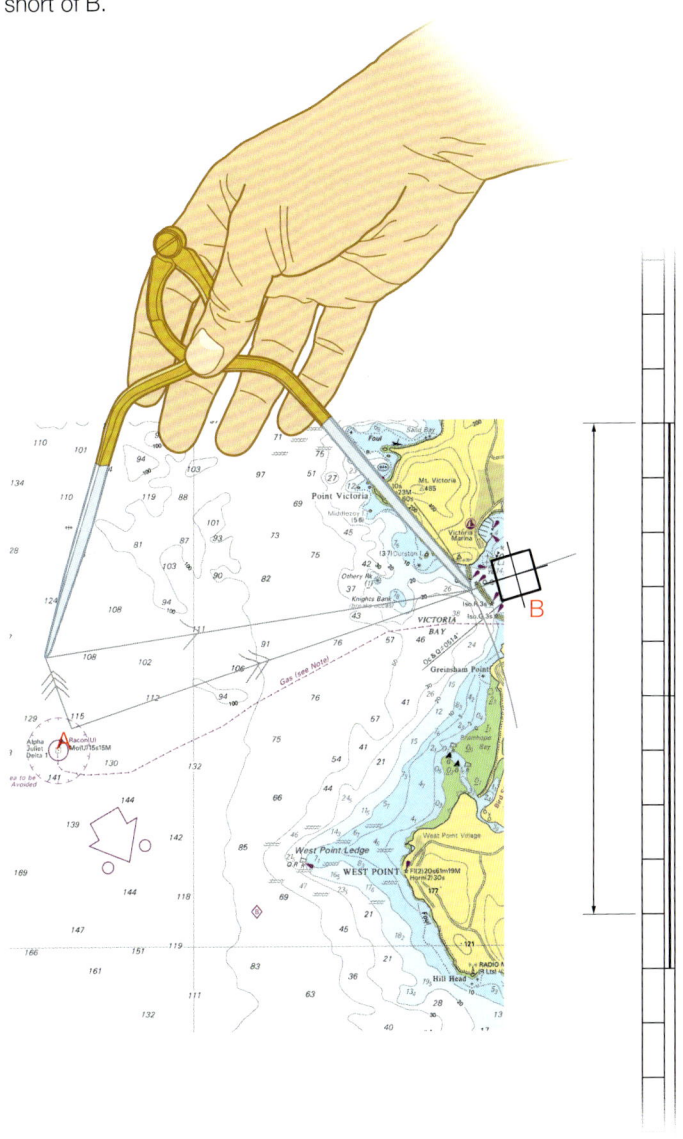

COURSE TO STEER

6 Measure direction of water track. This will be your course to steer.

= 061°(T)
  + 7°(W) variation
  ―――――――
  068°(M)

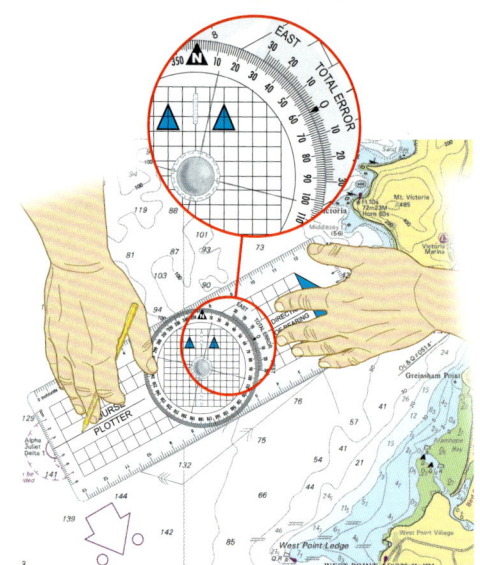

Applying Leeway

Taking your vessel's leeway into account becomes very important for long passages. You should head up into the wind by 5 to 10 degrees to compensate for your leeway. It is worth taking time to assess your leeway, but be careful to apply it in the correct way.

The example shows how applying just 4 degrees of leeway incorrectly puts a boat travelling at 5 knots over 2 miles off track in just three hours.

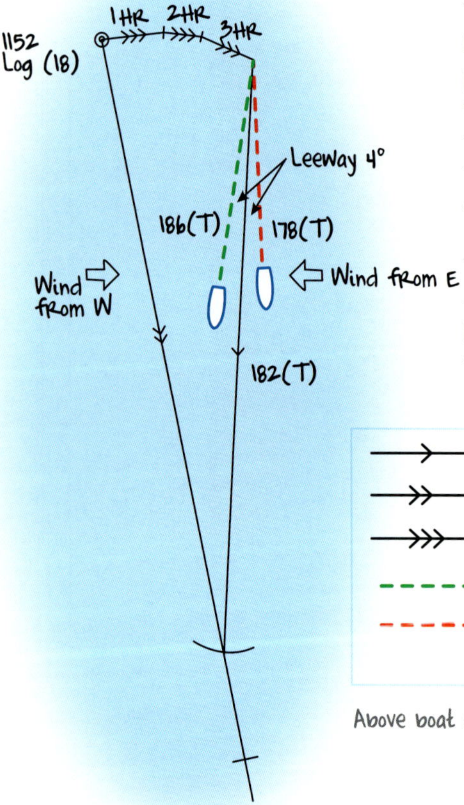

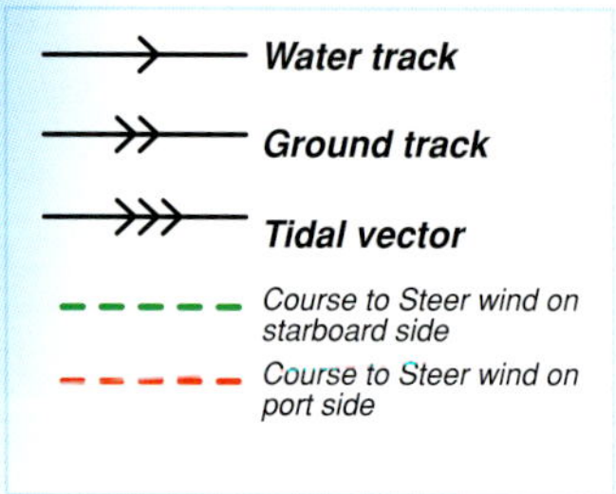

→ Water track
→→ Ground track
→→→ Tidal vector
- - - Course to Steer wind on starboard side
- - - Course to Steer wind on port side

Above boat @ 5 knots 8° difference = 2 miles off track

[56]

COURSE TO STEER

Calculating Estimated Time of Arrival (ETA)

You can work out your ETA to your destination. How long will it take to get from A to B?

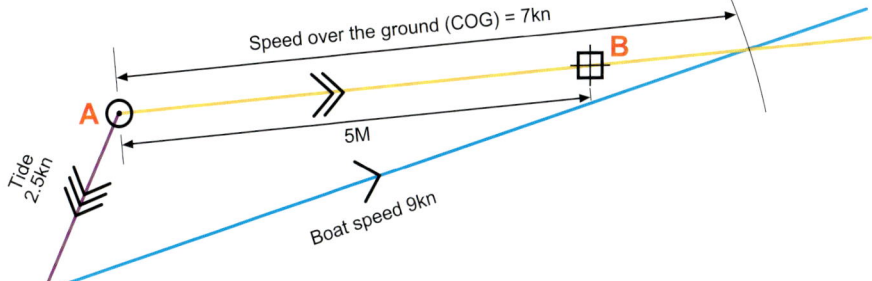

Use the DST triangle.
Time to your destination is calculated by distance/speed over ground.

5M / 7 knots = 0.71 hours
= 0.71 x 60 minutes
= 43 minutes

Vectors

If you estimate that your passage will take a little less than an hour – say 50 minutes...

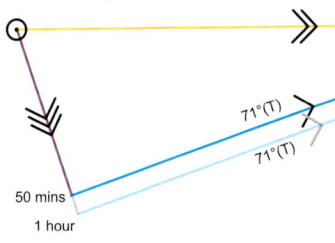

...avoid complicating your calculation by drawing a plot made from, say, 50 minutes of tide and 50 minutes of boat speed. As long as the predicted tide is constant your answer will be the same as for a one-hour plot.

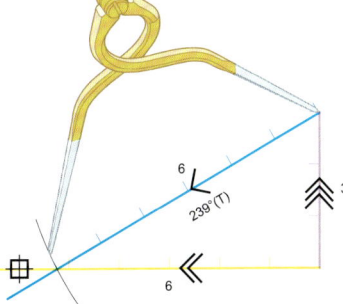

You should arc off the total distance you expect (boat speed x time) from the end of the tide to a point on the ground track.
E.T.A. = Start time + Duration.

Don't join the dots by drawing a line from the end of the tide to the destination.

[57]

COURSE TO STEER

When the Directions of the Tidal Streams are in Opposition

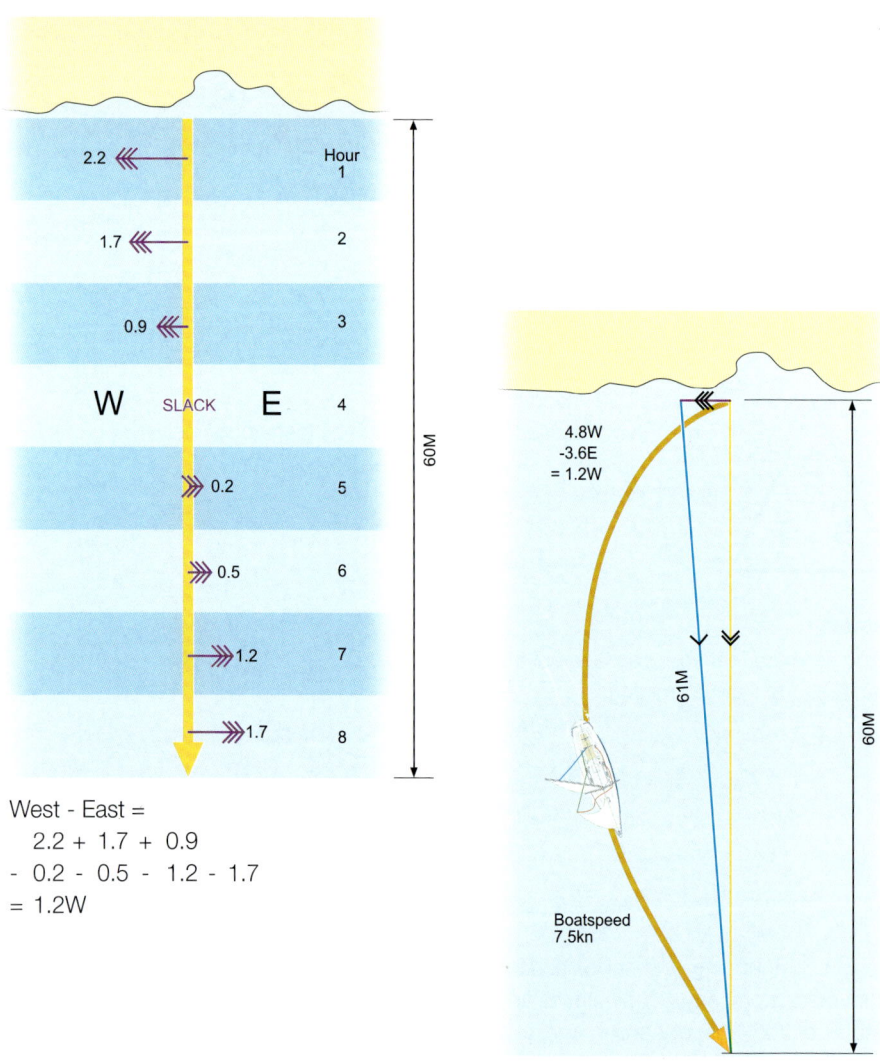

West − East =
  2.2 + 1.7 + 0.9
− 0.2 − 0.5 − 1.2 − 1.7
= 1.2W

Add up all the East- and West-going tidal streams and plot this as one vector. Arc off total distance to travel =
Total distance travelled = boat speed x time
= 7.5 knots x 8 hours
= 60M

COURSE TO STEER

When Tidal Streams change Direction every Hour

You must work out a tidal vector for each hour of passage.

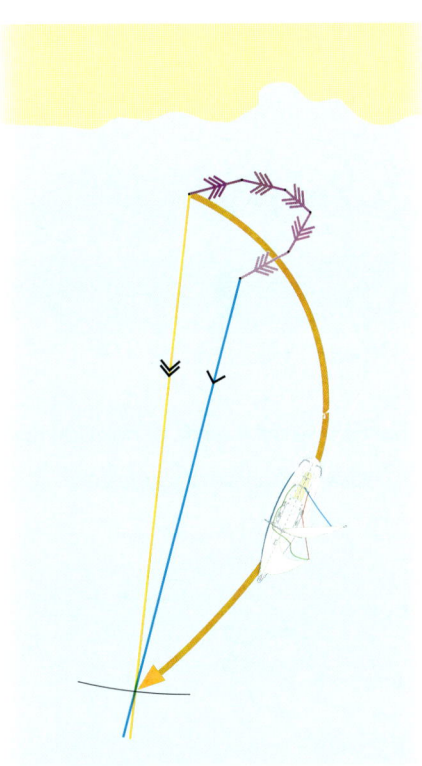

Plot a chain of vectors at the beginning of the ground track and then arc off the total distance to travel.

[59]

Rules of the Road

Rule 5

A proper lookout shall be kept at all times by sight and hearing and by all available means to appraise fully the risk of collision.

Beware of blind spots caused by sails/sprayhoods/dodgers etc.

Proceed at a safe speed and beware of faster vessels overtaking.

How can we tell if a risk of collision exists?

Rule 7

The collision regulations suggest that, if in doubt, you should monitor the bearing.

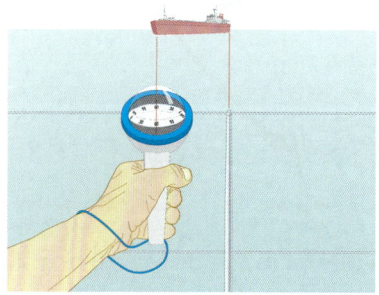

While on a steady course, take a bearing of the ship or line it up with a part of your boat/vessel such as a stanchion or stay.

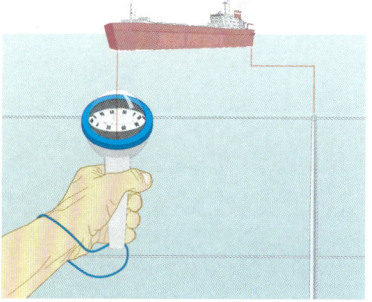

If the bearing of the ship changes or moves in relation to your stanchion there will not be a collision.

If the bearing stays steady or the ship remains lined up with your stanchion, a risk of collision exists.

RULES OF THE ROAD

Rule 7

The collision regulations state that radar shall be used if fitted.

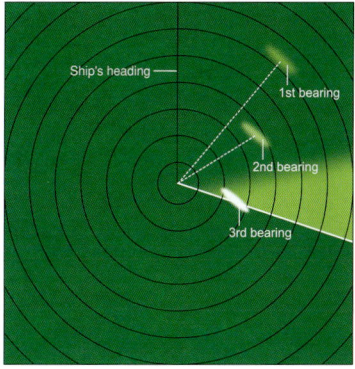

Increasing bearing should pass behind

If the bearing stays steady, a risk of collision exists.

Constant bearing risk of collision

To be proficient in the use of radar it should be used regularly in all conditions.

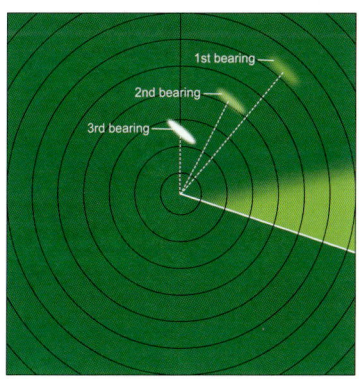

Decreasing bearing should pass in front

RULES OF THE ROAD

Order of Priority

The International Regulations for the Prevention of Collisions at Sea (IRPCS) is mostly common sense – a more manoeuvrable vessel must not impede a less manoeuvrable one.

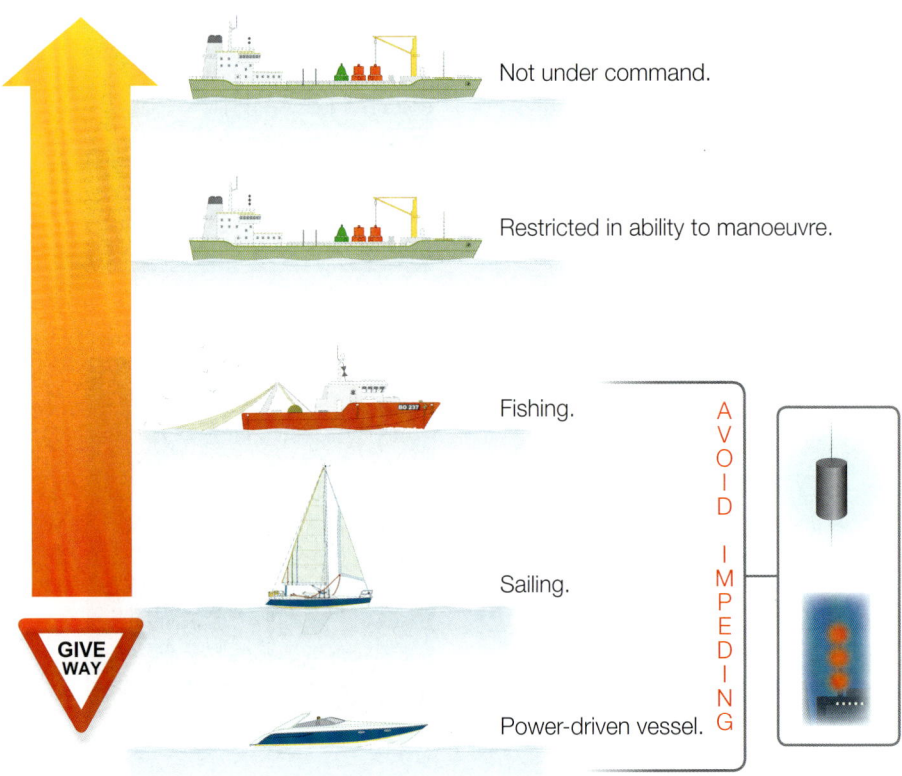

The above order of priority does not apply when the rules governing traffic separation schemes, narrow channels, or overtaking dictate otherwise.

RULES OF THE ROAD

Who Gives Way? – Power-driven Vessels

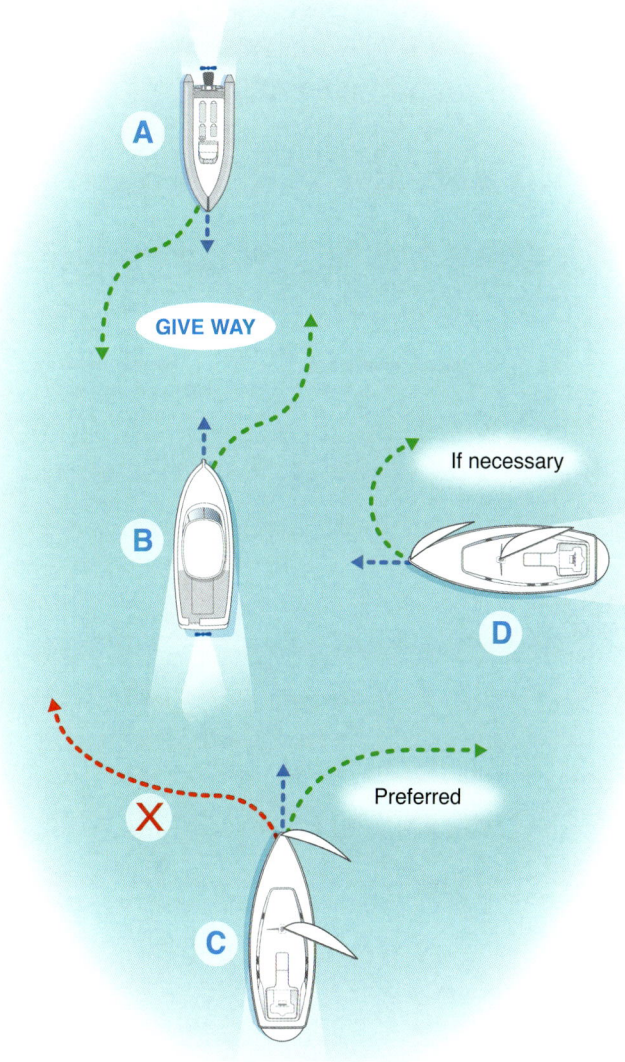

Vessels A and B need to give way by turning to starboard. Vessel C may need to give way to D by slowing down or preferably altering course to starboard. Vessel D is a stand-on vessel but should be prepared to take action if necessary.

RULES OF THE ROAD

Manoeuvring Signals

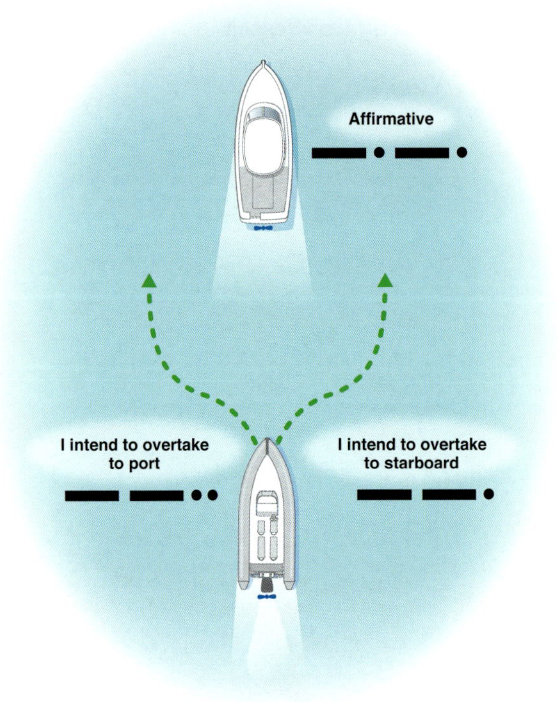

Affirmative
— • —

I intend to overtake to port
— — • •

I intend to overtake to starboard
— — • —

In sight of each other

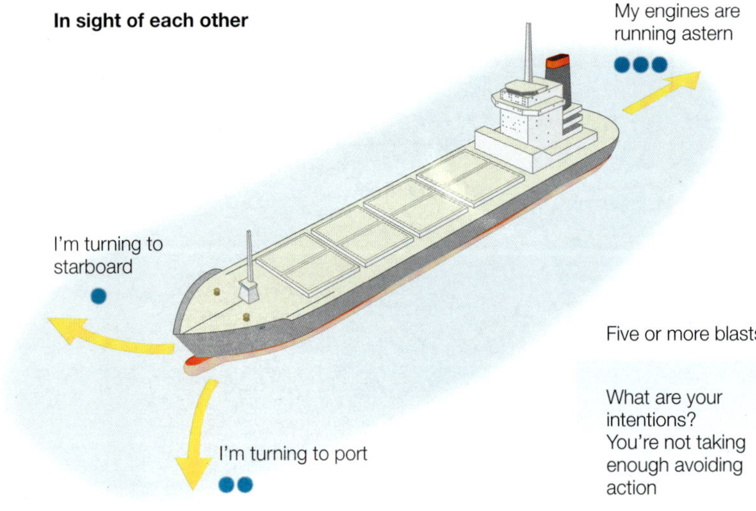

My engines are running astern
• • •

I'm turning to starboard
•

I'm turning to port
• •

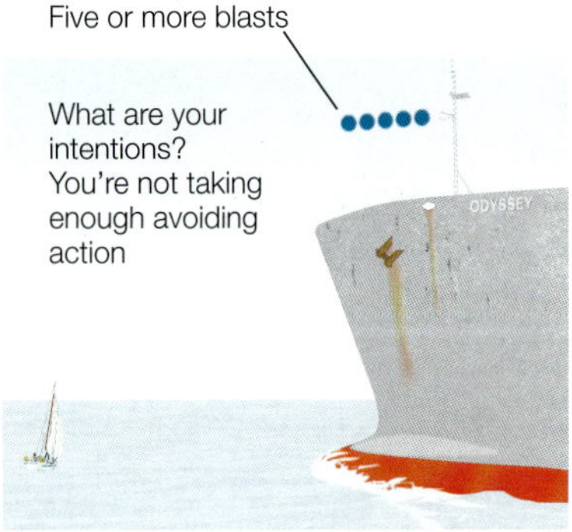

Five or more blasts
• • • • •

What are your intentions? You're not taking enough avoiding action

RULES OF THE ROAD

Avoiding Shipping – Traffic Separation Schemes

When crossing, make sure your heading, not your ground track, is at right angles to the TSS. Try to avoid crossing a TSS in fog or sailing across in light winds. You must try to cross as quickly as possible.

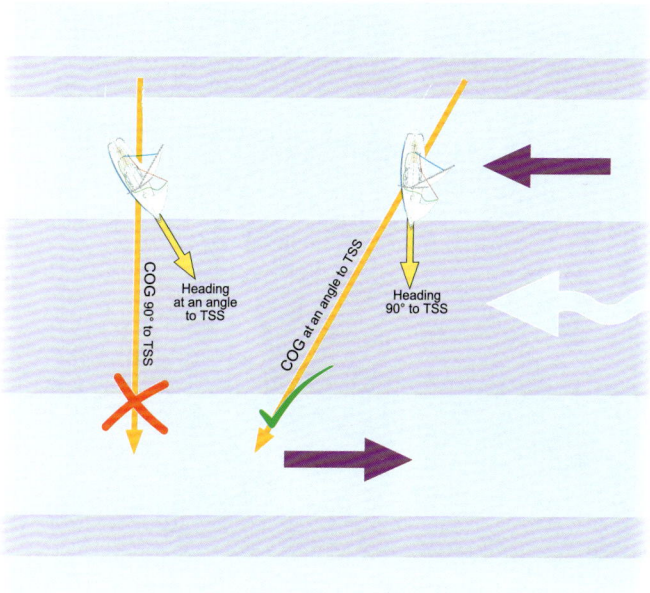

Narrow Channels

Larger vessels rely on keeping up their speed to be able to manoeuvre. Small vessels and sailing vessels should avoid impeding them.

Avoid anchoring in a narrow channel.

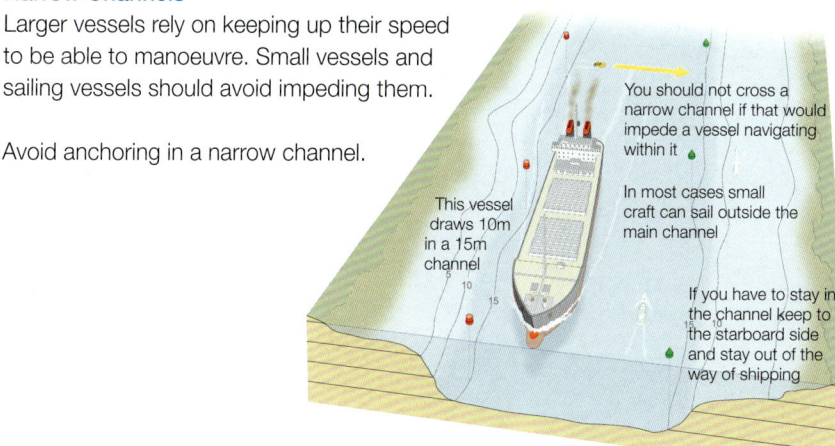

Vessel Lights, Shapes & Sound Signals in Restricted Visibility

Under sail
Less than 20m (vessels >70m must show separate side lights)

FOG

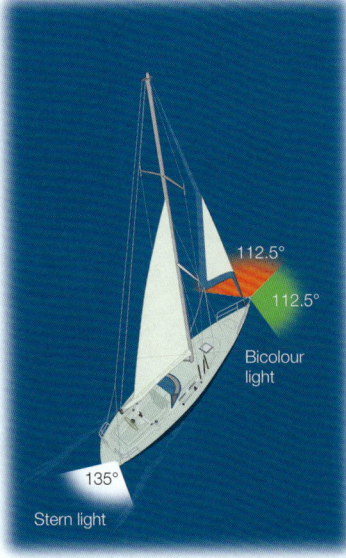

Power-driven vessels

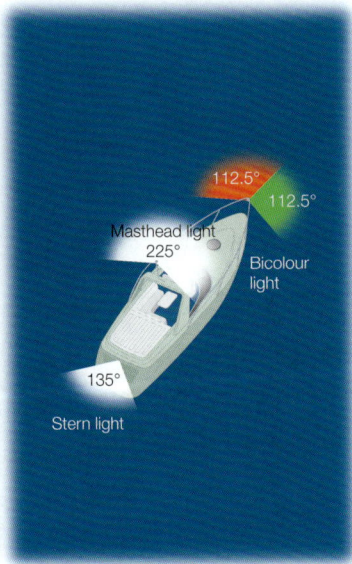

▬▬ • •

At least every two minutes.

▬▬

Making way.

▬▬ ▬▬

Under way but stopped, making no way.

At least every two minutes.

VESSEL LIGHTS, SHAPES & SOUND SIGNALS IN RESTRICTED VISIBILITY

Sailing vessel under power

By day

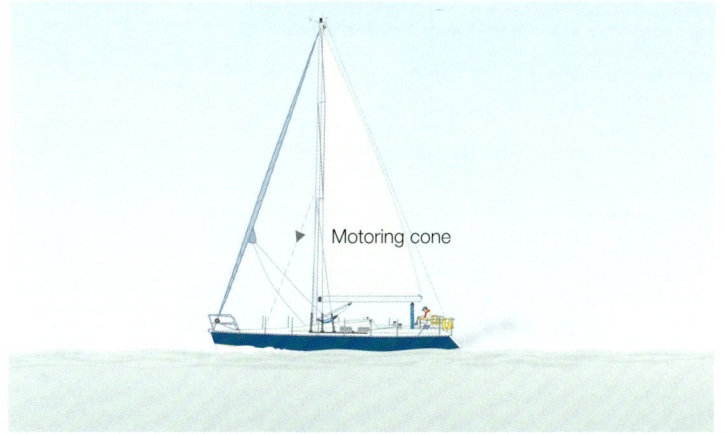

FOG

At night

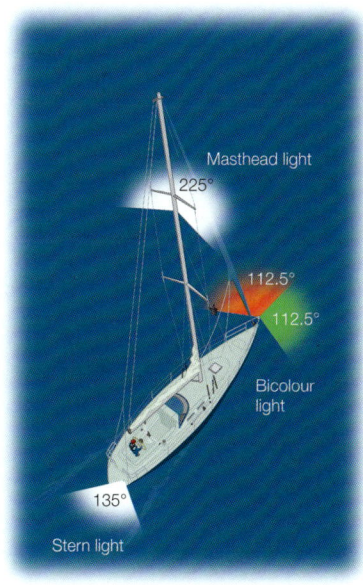
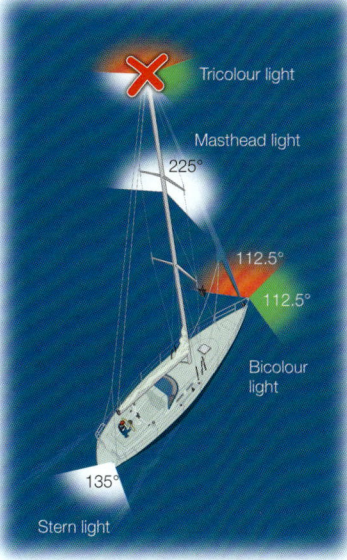

▬

Making way.

▬ ▬

Under way but stopped, making no way.

At least every two minutes.

VESSEL LIGHTS, SHAPES & SOUND SIGNALS IN RESTRICTED VISIBILITY

Larger ships (over 50m) must have two masthead lights.

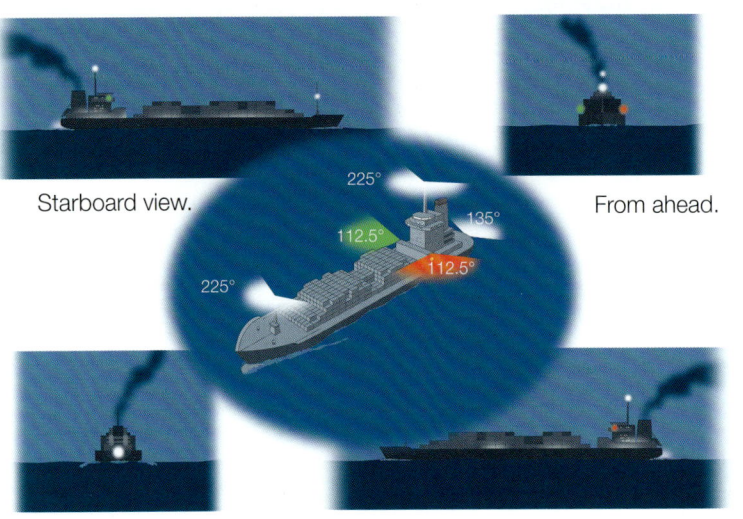

Starboard view.

From ahead.

From astern.

Port view.

FOG

Making way.

Under way but stopped, making no way.

At least every two minutes.

For a full explanation of collision regulations see the book G2 RYA International Regulations for Preventing Collisions at Sea.

At Anchor. >100m (illuminated deck).

By day.

FOG

Bell rung (bow) for five seconds, followed by gong (stern) for five seconds.

One minute.

At Anchor. <50m.

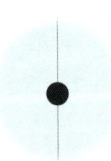

By day.

Bell rung for five seconds.

One minute.

VESSEL LIGHTS, SHAPES & SOUND SIGNALS IN RESTRICTED VISIBILITY

FOG

Bell rung (bow) for five seconds.

One minute.

At Anchor. >50m.
All anchored vessels may sound •▬• to warn approaching vessels of their position and potential collision.

By day.

By day.

FOG

Restricted in ability to manoeuvre.

E.g. dredging, cable laying etc

By day.

FOG

Carrying out underwater work.

Three all-round reds

E.g. large container ships or tankers in a narrow channel

By day.

Constrained by draught.

FOG

VESSEL LIGHTS, SHAPES & SOUND SIGNALS IN RESTRICTED VISIBILITY

Fishing by trawling.

By day.

FOG

Other types of fishing.

By day.

Vessel not under command.

By day.

FOG

Vessel aground.

By day.

Sound signal as per anchoring but with three distinct strokes on the bell immediately before and after the ringing of the bell.

VESSEL LIGHTS, SHAPES & SOUND SIGNALS IN RESTRICTED VISIBILITY

FOG

By day.

Towing – over 200m.

By day.

Tug:
▬ ● ●

Towing – from astern.

Tow (or last in tow):
▬ ● ● ●

Two minutes.

Towing – under 200m.

[71]

VESSEL LIGHTS, SHAPES & SOUND SIGNALS IN RESTRICTED VISIBILITY

FOG

Minesweeping.

By day.

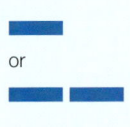

Air-cushion vessel.

VESSEL LIGHTS, SHAPES & SOUND SIGNALS IN RESTRICTED VISIBILITY

All round

On pilot duty.

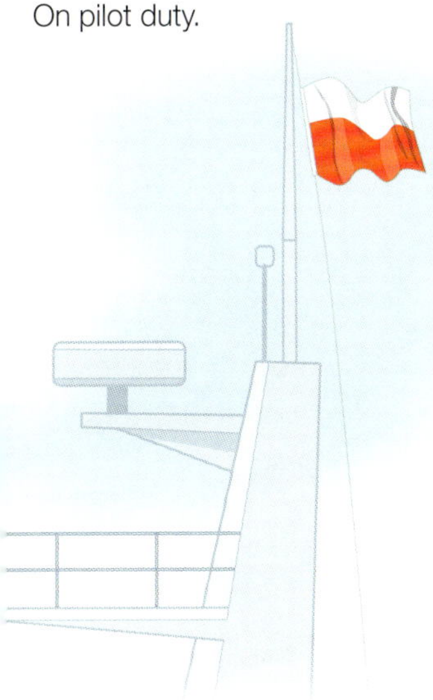

OR

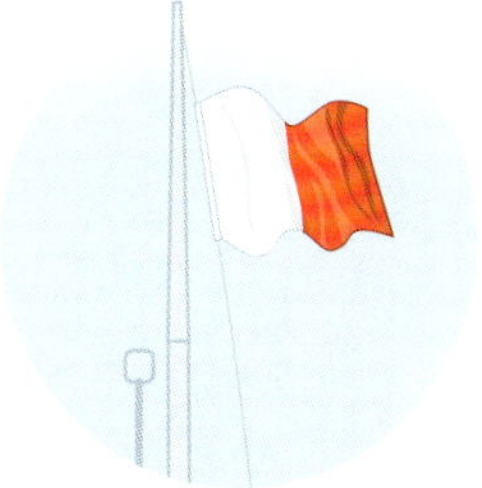

By day.

Both vertically and horizontally split red-and-white flags may be displayed by pilot vessels.

FOG

● ● ● ●

in addition to

▬

or

▬ ▬

or anchor sound.

By day.

Diving.

Safety Equipment

As skipper you are responsible for the safety of your crew, the condition of your vessel and all equipment on board!

It is advisable to take training courses in first aid, navigation and how to fire flares. You should also have a basic knowledge of how to make running repairs to your vessel while at sea.

Working navigation lights conforming to correct specifications

Fire blanket in the galley – do not stow directly above the cooker

Soft wood bungs for plugging broken skin fittings and holes, and a wooden mallet. These should always be kept together

Extra warps can be very useful

Bucket with sponge, bailer and hand bilge pump (useful for confined spaces)

High-visibility sheet with the boat's name, for identification from the air

Spare water and fuel with funnel

Red hand flares, red parachute flares, orange pinpoint flares and orange buoyant smoke.
All should be contained within a waterproof polybottle with the lid on at all times.
This will keep flares dry and protect them from accidental ignition

Comprehensive toolkit and sufficient knowledge, for safe use when making running repairs

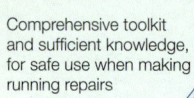

Powerful searchlight

Various engine spares – impeller, fuel filters, belts etc.

SAFETY EQUIPMENT

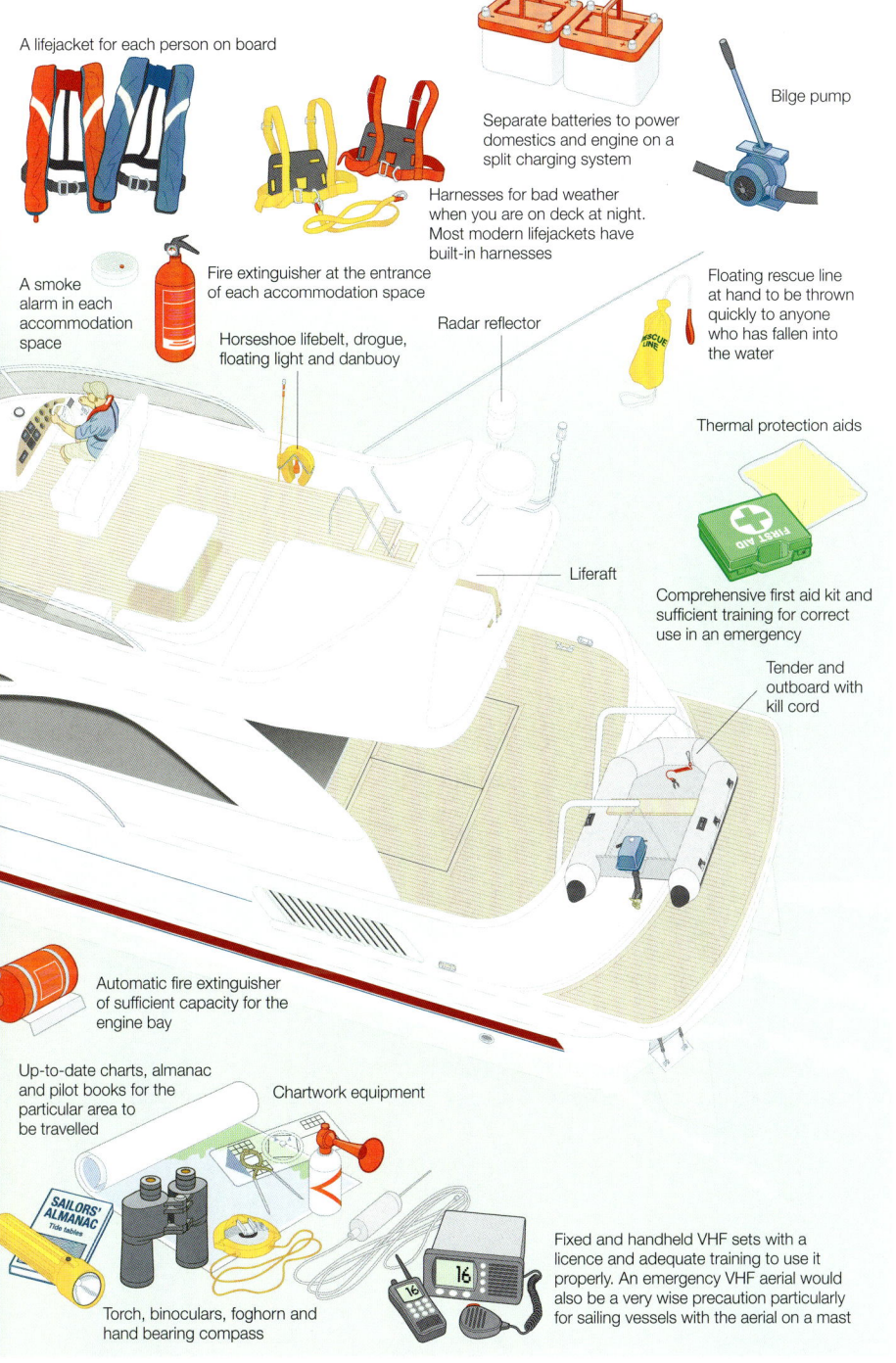

A lifejacket for each person on board

Separate batteries to power domestics and engine on a split charging system

Bilge pump

Harnesses for bad weather when you are on deck at night. Most modern lifejackets have built-in harnesses

A smoke alarm in each accommodation space

Fire extinguisher at the entrance of each accommodation space

Horseshoe lifebelt, drogue, floating light and danbuoy

Radar reflector

Floating rescue line at hand to be thrown quickly to anyone who has fallen into the water

Thermal protection aids

Liferaft

Comprehensive first aid kit and sufficient training for correct use in an emergency

Tender and outboard with kill cord

Automatic fire extinguisher of sufficient capacity for the engine bay

Up-to-date charts, almanac and pilot books for the particular area to be travelled

Chartwork equipment

Torch, binoculars, foghorn and hand bearing compass

Fixed and handheld VHF sets with a licence and adequate training to use it properly. An emergency VHF aerial would also be a very wise precaution particularly for sailing vessels with the aerial on a mast

[75]

Stability

Stability is an area of naval architecture that covers how a vessel behaves at sea. In addition to the initial design and construction of the vessel, sea state, weather conditions, and weight distribution all have an effect on the behaviour of the vessel at sea. The wrong combination of these factors can make life at sea uncomfortable and in extreme cases dangerous.

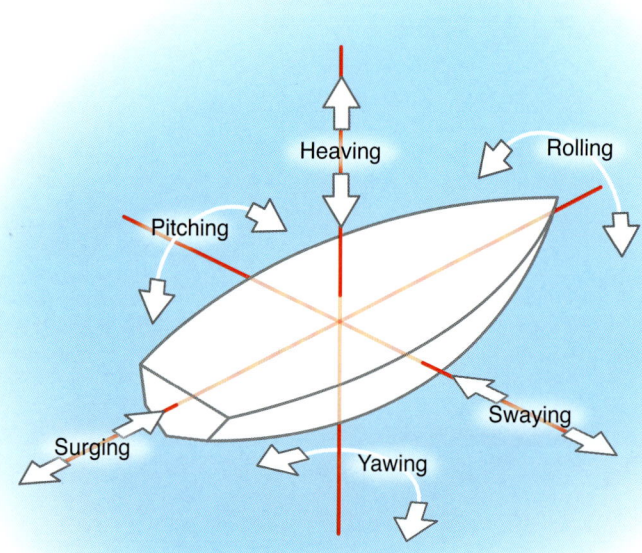

The movement of a vessel at sea can be described in six ways:
- In straight lines: surging forwards and back; heaving up and down; swaying to the port and starboard.
- At angles: rolling to port and starboard; pitching forward and aft; yawing to port and starboard.

STABILITY

As a boat heels, B moves away from G, creating a righting moment called GZ.

Righting Moment Curve

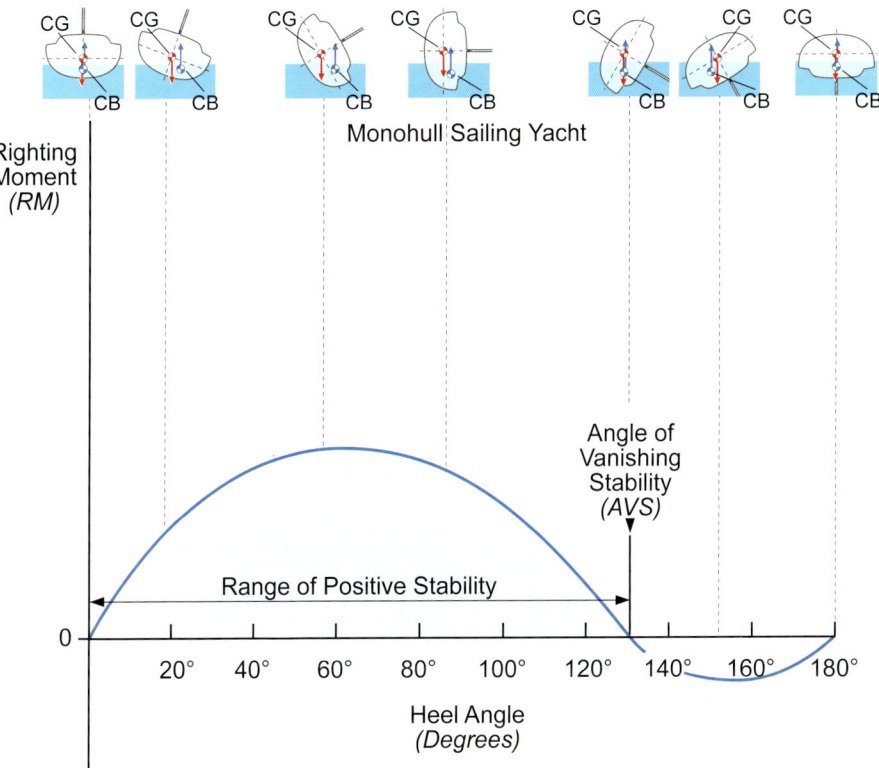

Manufacturers produce righting moment curves to show the stability characteristics of their boats. The higher the AVS, the more likely a vessel is:
- to resist becoming inverted
- to return to upright after being inverted.

A heavy boat takes more energy to heel because:
energy = boat weight (force) x GZ (distance) = RM (righting moment).

STABILITY

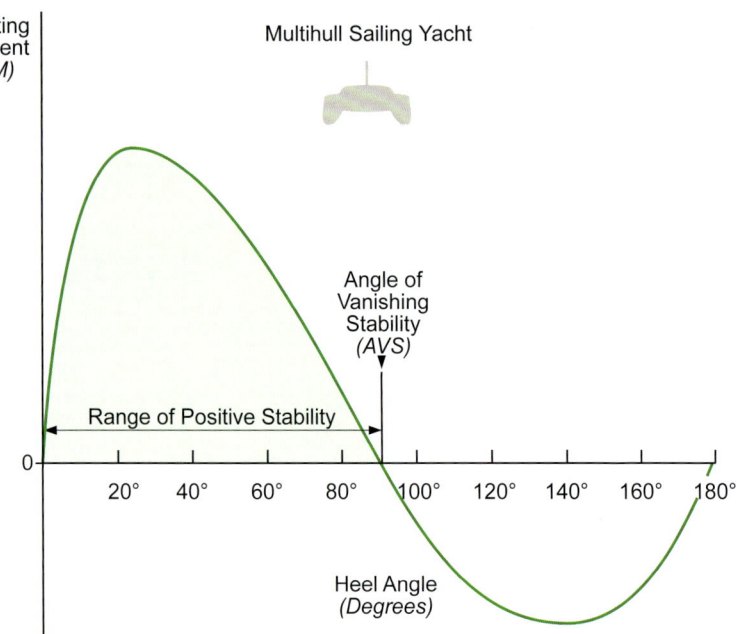

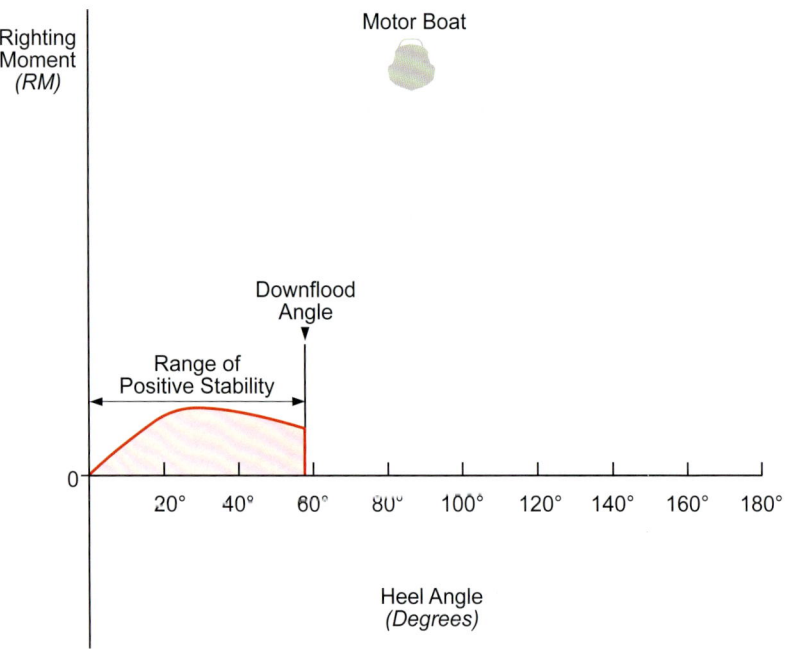

STABILITY

Raising Centre of Gravity

In the diagram to the right the boat has an 80kg weight on the top of the mast. This raises its centre of gravity so much that the vessel is unstable when upright, and so leans to one side until the righting moment of buoyancy counteracts the force from the weight. This unstable leaning is called lolling. It is quite different to a yacht heeling due to external forces such as a strong wind.

It is worth noting that when a weight is hoisted from the top of a mast the effect on the boat is the same as if the weight is at the top of the mast. This can seriously affect a vessel's stability as soon as the weight is lifted off the deck.

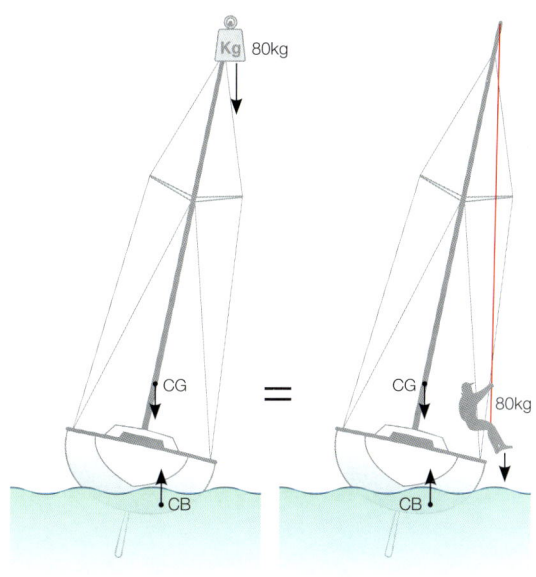

CG = Centre of Gravity
CB = Centre of Buoyancy

Adding weight aloft will raise the centre of gravity and lower your AVS.

Breaking waves release large amounts of energy related to their size, which may be sufficient to invert small yachts.

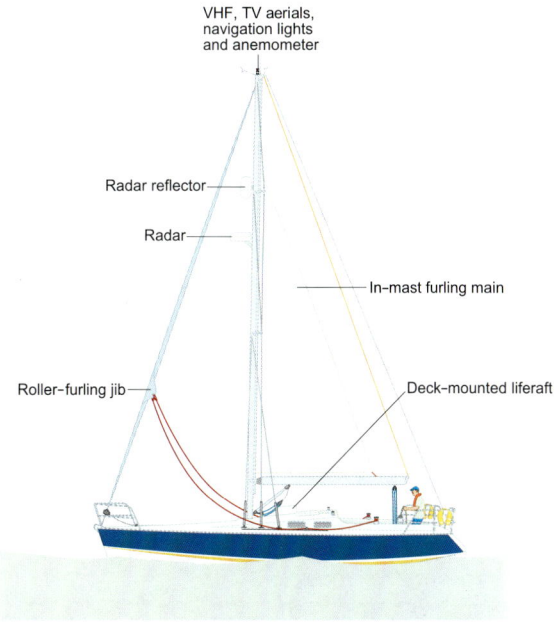

[79]

STABILITY

Sea State

A yacht is most likely to be rolled when beam-on to a large breaking wave.

When caught beam-on, a breaking wave the same height as the beam of your vessel is sufficient to cause it to invert.

Be aware of the limits of your boat when undertaking passages in rough weather and/or where you might encounter breaking waves, e.g. tidal overfalls etc.

Free-surface Effect

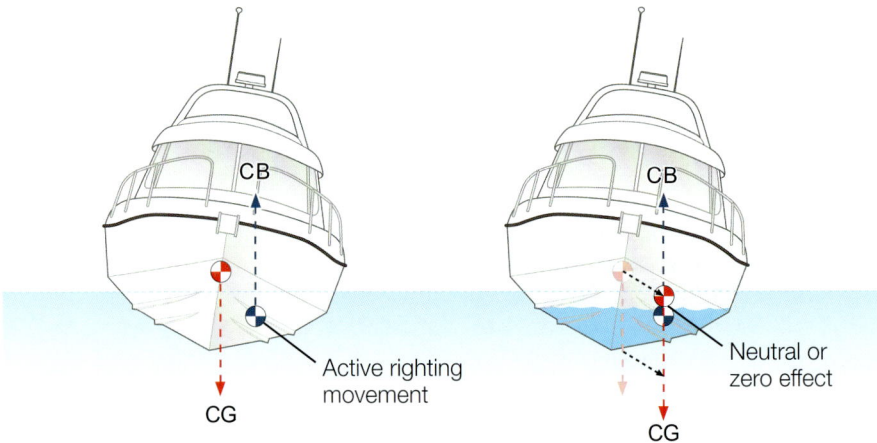

Free-surface effect allows the mass of water in a boat to move its centre of gravity. In this example, the AVS is reduced to 15 degrees by the mass of water in the bilges.

In rough weather, small amounts of water finding their way into a vessel over a period of time can accumulate alarmingly. One litre every 10 seconds equals 1,080 litres (over a tonne) every three hours!

STABILITY

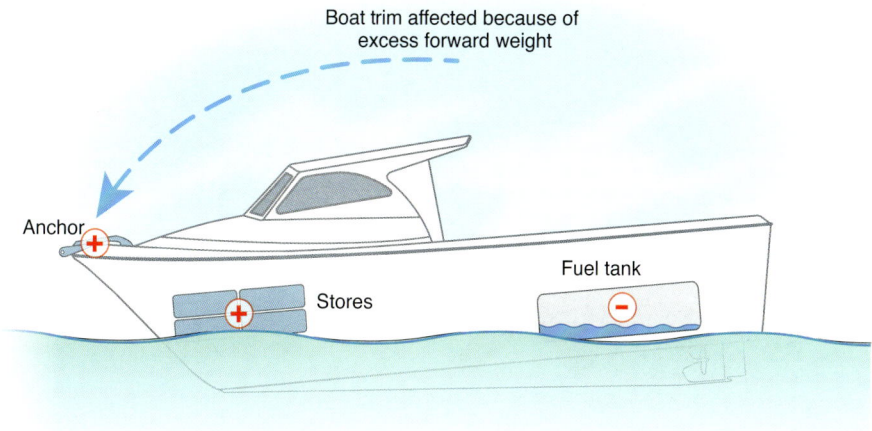

Managing where your weight (e.g. stores, sails, tanks for water and fuel) is located is important. It needs to be managed on a passage to minimise negative impact on stability. When sea state and weather affect stability, boat speed, sail plan, course, trim tabs etc., have maximum effect.

Recreational Craft Directive

New yachts in Europe are built to the Recreational Craft Directive, which lays down minimum standards for construction and stability. It gives an indication of the operating limits of a vessel with the category A, B, C, or D displayed on the builder's plate.

Category	Wind	*Significant Wave Height*
A Ocean	>F8	>4m
B Offshore	<F8	<4m
C Inshore	<F6	<2m
D Sheltered Waters	<F4	<0.5m

Note: Some waves may be twice this height.

Significant wave height is the average wave height of the largest third of waves observed, so some waves experienced will be larger than the significant wave height listed.

Fire Safety

Common Causes of Fire

Smoking below decks.

Solvents/paints stored below.

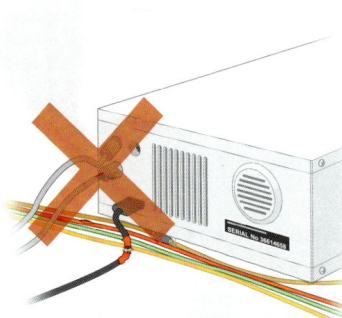

Faulty wiring.

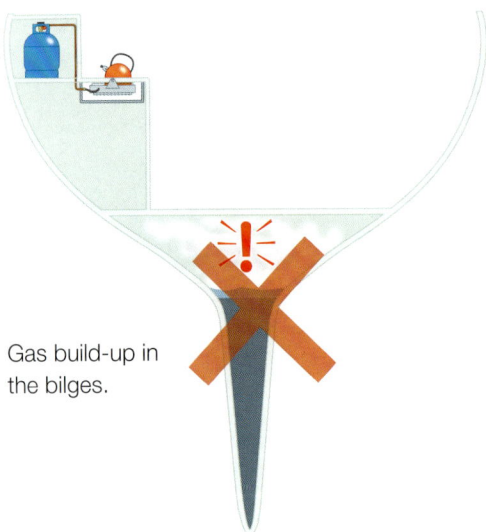

Gas build-up in the bilges.

Cooking fats.

FIRE SAFETY

Extinguishers

	Class A Fires (Paper, wood etc.)	Class B Fires (Flammable Liquids)	Class C Fires (Flammable Gas Fires)	Class D Fires (Metal Fires)	Class E Fires (Electrical Fires)
Foam (Cream)	✓	✓			✗
CO_2 (Black)		✓ (Secondary)			✓ (Primary)
Powder (Blue)	✓	✓	✓	✓	✓

Blanket – good for smothering flames and if clothing is on fire.

Petrol/Gasoline Vapour

Always vent engine space before starting an inboard petrol engine.

Keep outboards on deck to avoid the build-up of petrol vapour below.

Gas Safety

Butane and propane can be highly dangerous.

To clear gas, open hatches and turn downwind to vent fresh air through the boat.

Bilge pumps are designed to pump water, but may be effective for low volumes of gas. Many won't clear gas very effectively. Use of electric bilge pumps should be avoided if a gas leak is suspected.

Don't attempt DIY repairs to your system. Always call in a qualified fitter.

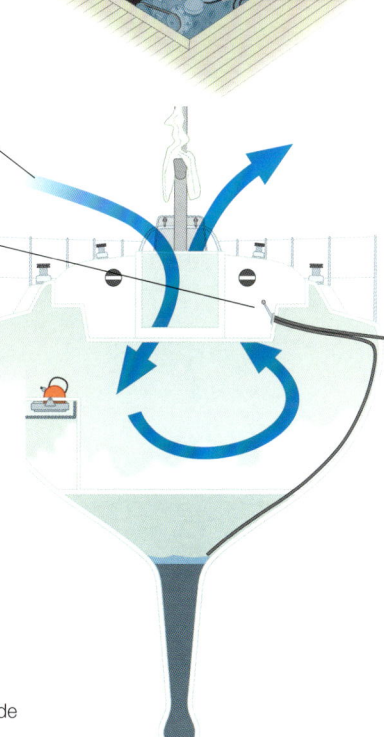

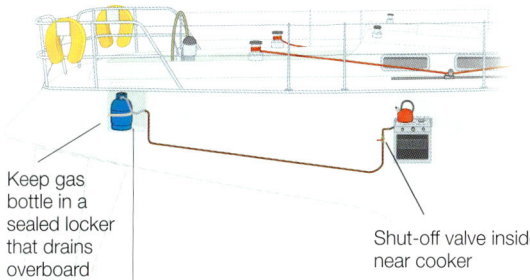

Keep gas bottle in a sealed locker that drains overboard

Shut-off valve inside near cooker

Drainage hole

Fire Fighting & Fire Prevention

Location of Extinguishers

Extinguishers should be to hand near the exit to each accommodation space.

The engine space should have its own dedicated extinguisher which is automatic or can be activated remotely without having to open the engine compartment and let in oxygen.

FIRE FIGHTING & FIRE PREVENTION

Fighting the Fire

If you cannot fight the fire, be prepared to abandon ship.

Remember: The boat will fill up with smoke very quickly. Get everyone on deck with a lifejacket. You may have to send a Mayday/fire distress flares etc.

Aim the extinguisher at the base of the flames.

Splashing water from a bucket can be more effective than throwing its entire contents at once.

Fire blankets can be used to smother a galley fire. Protect your hands when using a fire blanket.

They are also essential for clothing fires.

Distress Signals

Flares

Never fire a parachute rocket if a helicopter is approaching.

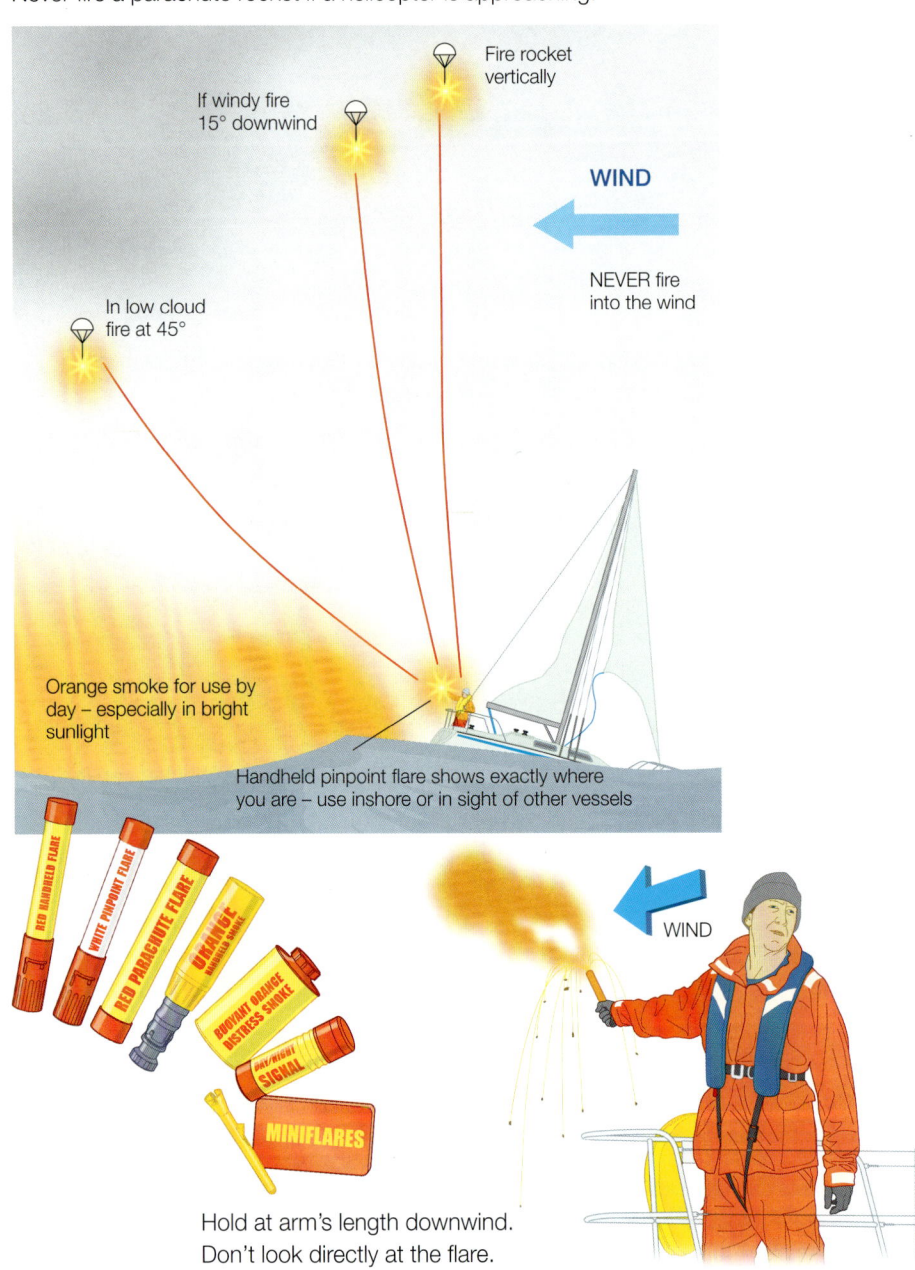

Fire rocket vertically

If windy fire 15° downwind

WIND

NEVER fire into the wind

In low cloud fire at 45°

Orange smoke for use by day – especially in bright sunlight

Handheld pinpoint flare shows exactly where you are – use inshore or in sight of other vessels

WIND

Hold at arm's length downwind.
Don't look directly at the flare.

DISTRESS SIGNALS

Other Distress Signals

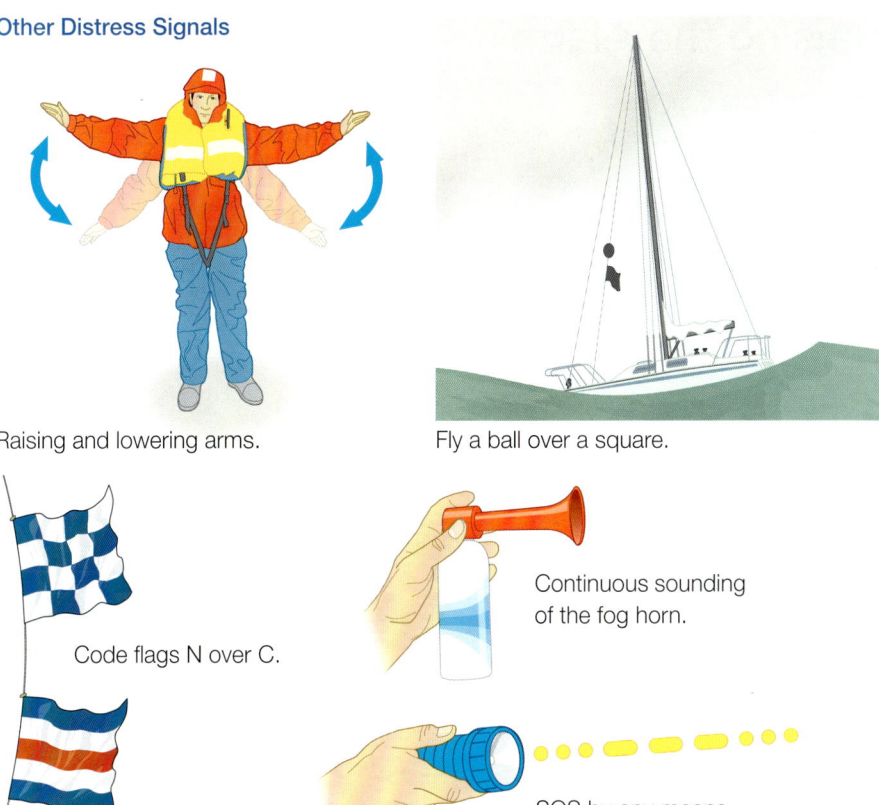

Raising and lowering arms.

Fly a ball over a square.

Code flags N over C.

Continuous sounding of the fog horn.

SOS by any means.

SART
A Search and Rescue Radar Transponder shows your position on another boat's radar. It is not good at alerting, but it is good for locating.

AIS SART
A modern version of SART using the VHF frequencies of the Automatic Identification System.

EPIRB
Emergency Position Indicating Radio Beacon – when activated it sends a distress message to the rescue services via a satellite system. Your position is then pinpointed. You must register your EPIRB with the coastguard.

Personal Beacons
PLBs: Similar to EPIRB, sometimes called Personal EPIRBs. Useful for alerting but not helpful for a vessel carrying out MOB.
AIS Locator Beacons: Similar to AIS SARTs. Useful for MOB. Limited alerting.

Raising the Alarm

VHF VOICE CALL
Use VHF to alert the coastguard and other vessels in your area. You must tell them:

- your boat's name
- your position
- how many people are on board
- what assistance you require.

VHF is better than a mobile phone for distress calling. Other vessels in your area will hear your call and the coastguard can use VHF transmissions to fix your position.

A mobile phone will only tell one person that you are in trouble. The network coverage is patchy away from land and you won't be able to talk directly to a helicopter or lifeboat.

DIGITAL VHF (DSC) CALL
You may not have time to send a voice call but some modern VHF sets can:

- send a distress alert or urgency call at the press of a button
- be linked to a GNSS to give your position.

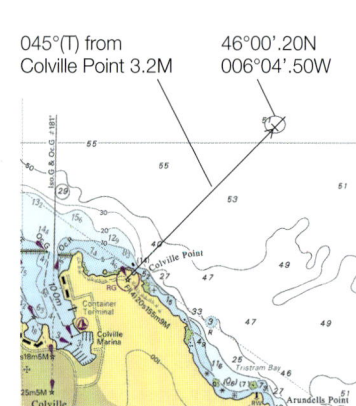

045°(T) from   46°00'.20N
Colville Point 3.2M   006°04'.50W

RAISING THE ALARM

MAYDAY

When life or vessel are in grave and imminent danger.

> Mayday x 3
>
> This is... (yacht name spoken three times)
>
> (Call sign and MMSI number (if you have DSC))
>
> Mayday
>
> (Yacht name, call sign and MMSI number)
>
> Position is... (Give position in either latitude and longitude or distance and bearing from a charted object)
>
> Nature of Distress (Describe briefly what the problem is, for example sinking, MOB, boat on fire, stranded)
>
> I require immediate assistance
>
> Number of people on board (including yourself)
>
> Further information (Anything that may help rescuers, such as abandoning to liferaft, triggered EPIRB, etc.)
>
> Over (the invitation to reply)

PAN PAN

Urgency message – if crew or vessel needs assistance.

> Pan Pan (Three times)
>
> All stations (Three times)
>
> This is... (name of boat x 3 (call sign +MMSI if fitted with DSC))
>
> Position is... (Give position in latitude and longitude or distance and bearing from a charted object)
>
> Nature of problem (e.g. broken down and in need of a tow)
>
> Number of persons on board (including yourself)
>
> Over

You may use a VHF radio under the supervision of a qualified person or to make a distress call – otherwise you need an operator's certificate.
Contact the RYA or your national maritime authority for details of courses.

Emergency Procedures

Boating is generally a safe pastime but, should the worst happen, make sure you and your crew know what to do.

If you are not already wearing one, put on a lifejacket.

Alert the coastguard.

Use a pinpoint flare (night) or an orange smoke (day).

Abandoning to the liferaft

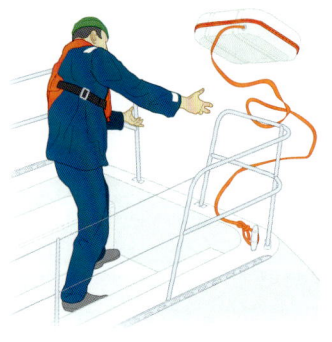

Throw to leeward and tug painter to inflate. Make sure the painter is tied on.

Board raft from the yacht. Stay dry. Put heaviest, strongest crew in first to stabilise the raft and assist others in boarding.

Once aboard:
- Cut painter
- Paddle away
- Stream drogue
- Close door
- Take seasickness tablets
- Keep as warm and dry as possible
- Ventilate interior every hour.

Rescue

The lifeboat coxswain will need to talk to you to assess the situation.

Make sure there are no lines in the water which could foul the lifeboat's propeller.

Any casualties will be taken off.

You may be taken in tow but the lifeboat's priority is to save lives, not salvage boats. Attach tow line to strong points via a bridle.

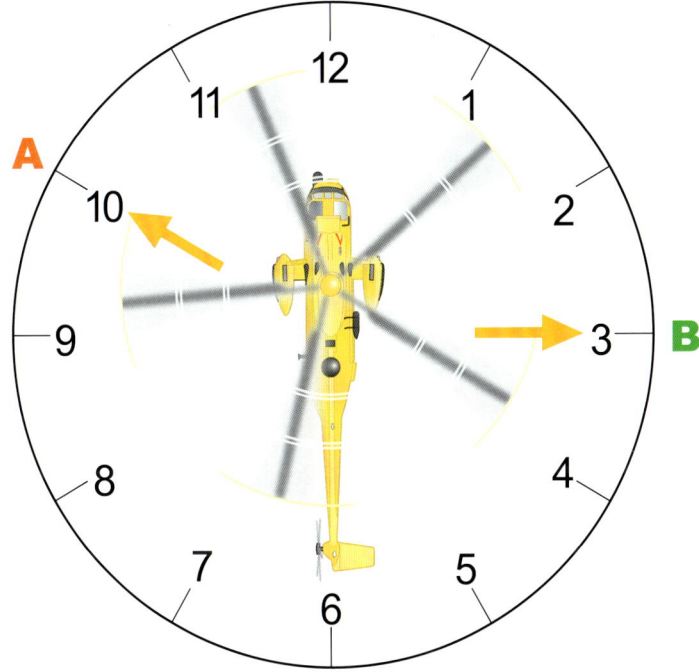

You will probably see or hear the helicopter before they see you. Call them on *VHF Channel 16* and give them your position and distance, *in relation to the helicopter*, using the clock notation above (for example, if you were 'A', "I am at your 10 o'clock" or 'B' "I am at your 3 o'clock"), even if you have triggered an EPIRB (121.5MHz) for them to home in on. Use a pinpoint flare (at night) or orange smoke (daytime) for them to locate your position from a distance once they know which direction to look.

Buoyage

IALA – Maritime Buoyage System

Two buoyage systems, IALA A and IALA B, exist in the world. The difference affects the colour and light characteristics of lateral marks. IALA A is used in Europe, Africa, Russia, India, Australia, and New Zealand. IALA B is used in the USA, South America, parts of the Caribbean, South-East Asia, and Canada.

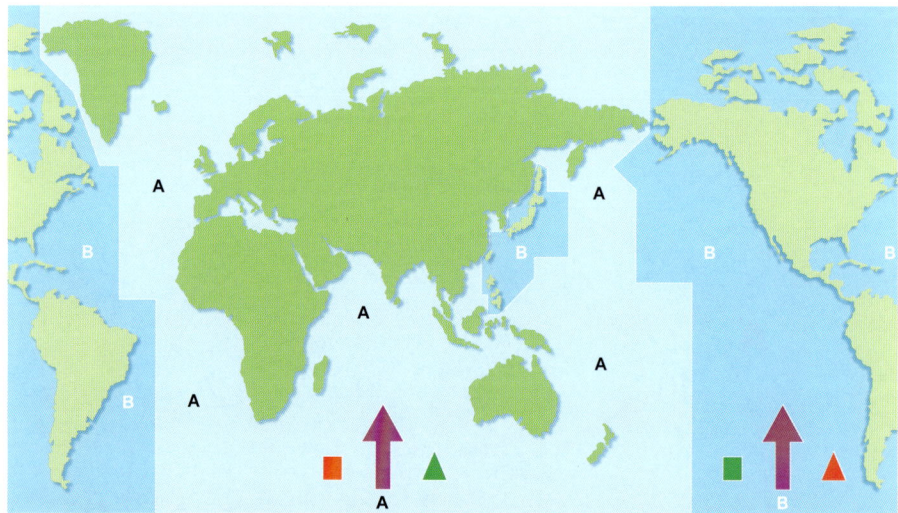

Six groups, each with different lights, colour, and rhythm: 1 Lateral (A/B). 2 Cardinal. 3 Isolated Danger. 4 Safe water. 5 Special. 6 Wreck.

Light Characteristics

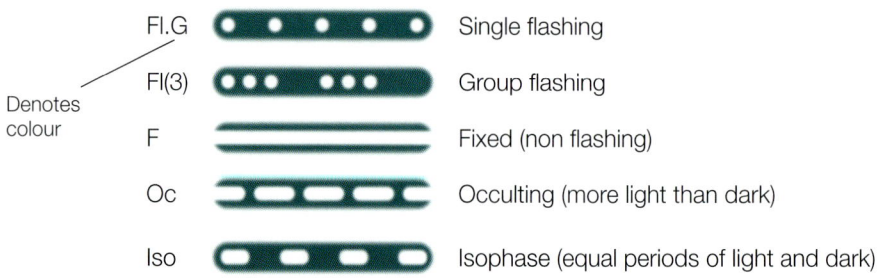

BUOYAGE

Lateral Marks

Used to mark channels.
Leave starboard cone to your starboard side when going into harbour.

Port Can
flashes red
– any rhythm
except 2+1

Starboard Cone
flashes green
– any rhythm
except 2+1

IALA A

Port Can
flashes green
– any rhythm
except 2+1

Starboard Cone
flashes red
– any rhythm
except 2+1

IALA B

Preferred Channel Marks (IALA A)

Preferred channel mark, may be placed where a channel splits in two, indicating the preferred channel.

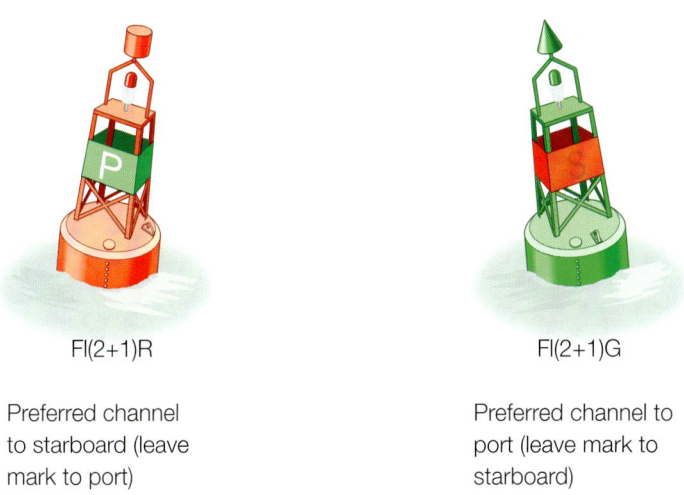

Fl(2+1)R

Preferred channel to starboard (leave mark to port)

Fl(2+1)G

Preferred channel to port (leave mark to starboard)

In IALA B, preferred channel marks have the opposite colours and lights, i.e. preferred channel to starboard is a green can with a red horizontal stripe. Light is Fl(2+1)G.

BUOYAGE

CARDINAL MARKS

CARDINALS

Cardinal marks indicate which side of the mark is safe water and remain constant throughout the IALA system. Cones point to black bands. Buoys are found in many shapes and sizes. Solar panels and lights can make top marks difficult to distinguish. Weeds and guano can alter the appearance and colour.

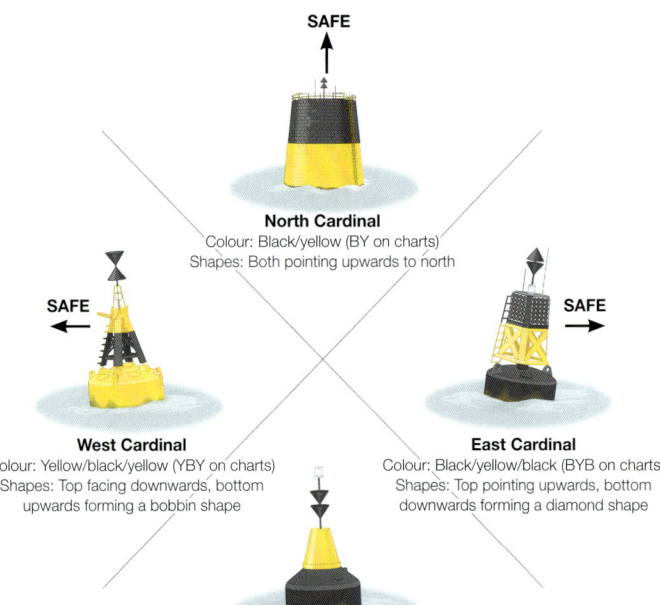

North Cardinal
Colour: Black/yellow (BY on charts)
Shapes: Both pointing upwards to north

West Cardinal
Colour: Yellow/black/yellow (YBY on charts)
Shapes: Top facing downwards, bottom upwards forming a bobbin shape

East Cardinal
Colour: Black/yellow/black (BYB on charts)
Shapes: Top pointing upwards, bottom downwards forming a diamond shape

South Cardinal
Colour: Yellow/black (YB on charts)
Shapes: Both pointing downwards to south

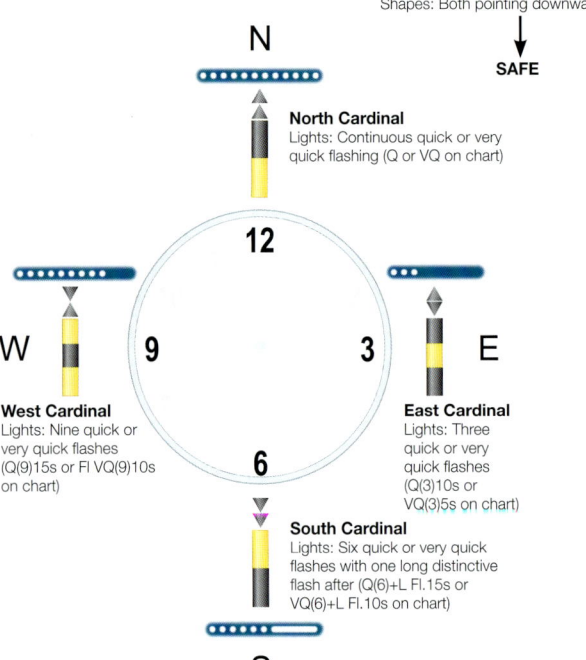

North Cardinal
Lights: Continuous quick or very quick flashing (Q or VQ on chart)

West Cardinal
Lights: Nine quick or very quick flashes (Q(9)15s or Fl VQ(9)10s on chart)

East Cardinal
Lights: Three quick or very quick flashes (Q(3)10s or VQ(3)5s on chart)

South Cardinal
Lights: Six quick or very quick flashes with one long distinctive flash after (Q(6)+L Fl.15s or VQ(6)+L Fl.10s on chart)

BUOYAGE

Isolated Danger

Fl(2)

Used to mark the exact location of an isolated hazard such as a wreck. Flashing white as a group of two.

Safe Water

One long flash, isophase, occulting or morse A

Used at the start of a buoyed channel.

Emergency Wreck-marking Buoy

Al.Oc.BuY.3s

Emergency wreck-marking buoy, placed at the site of a new wreck. Remains in place until the wreck has been dealt with.

Special Marks

Yellow, any rhythm other than those used for white lights in the vicinity

Used for a variety of purposes e.g. oceanographic buoys, personal watercraft areas, racing marks, etc.

BUOYAGE

IALA A Buoyage

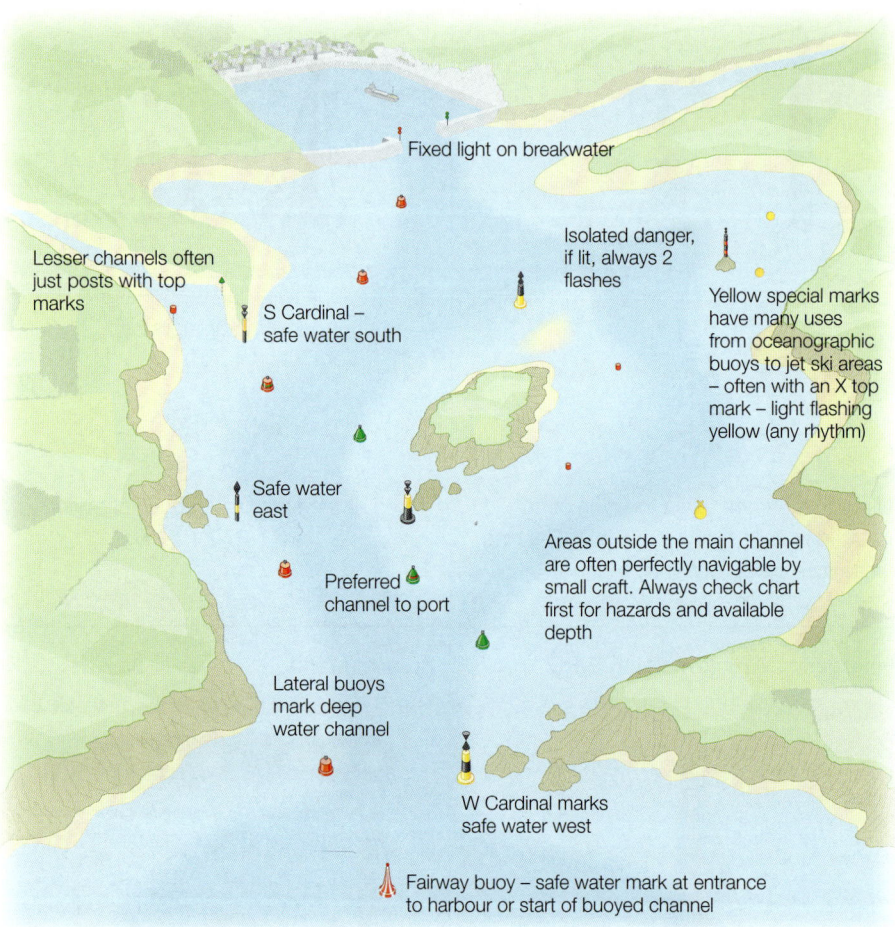

BUOYAGE

IALA B Buoyage

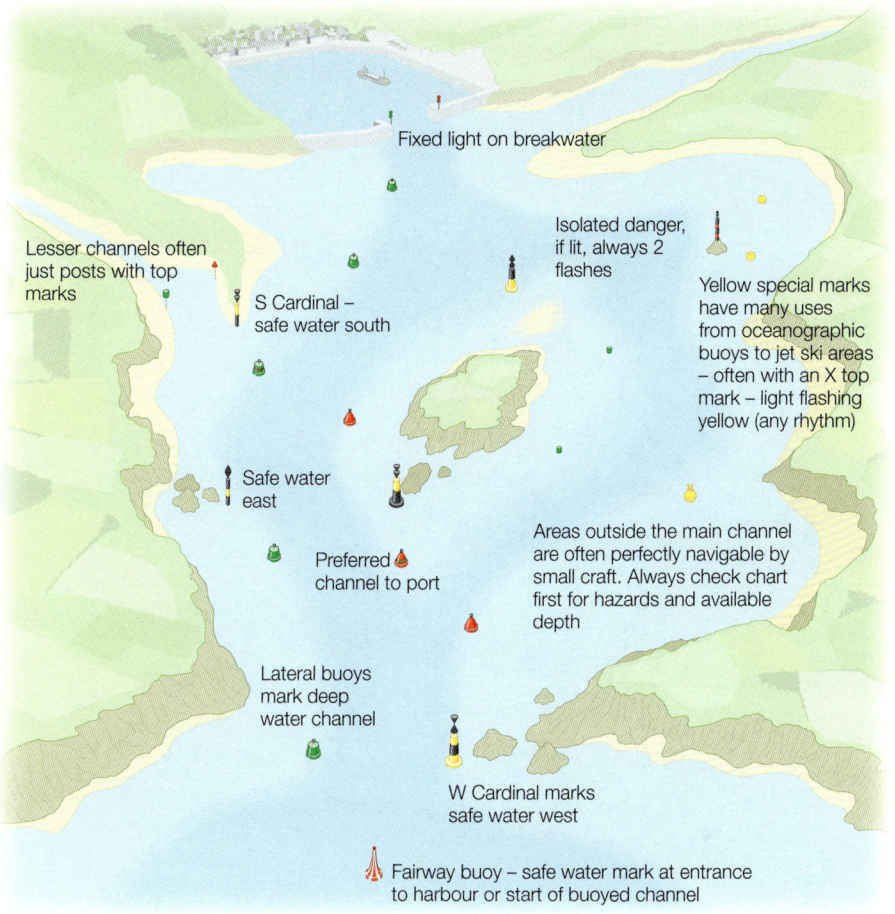

Sector Lights

Sector lights are designed to help you avoid danger by casting a sector of coloured light over a hazard or dangerous approach.

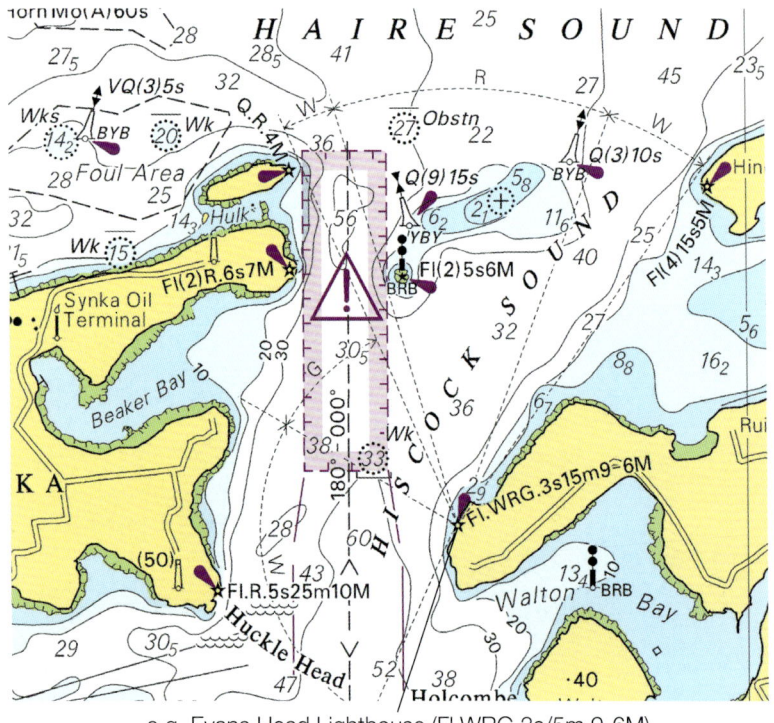

e.g. Evans Head Lighthouse (Fl.WRG.3s/5m 9-6M)

SECTOR LIGHTS

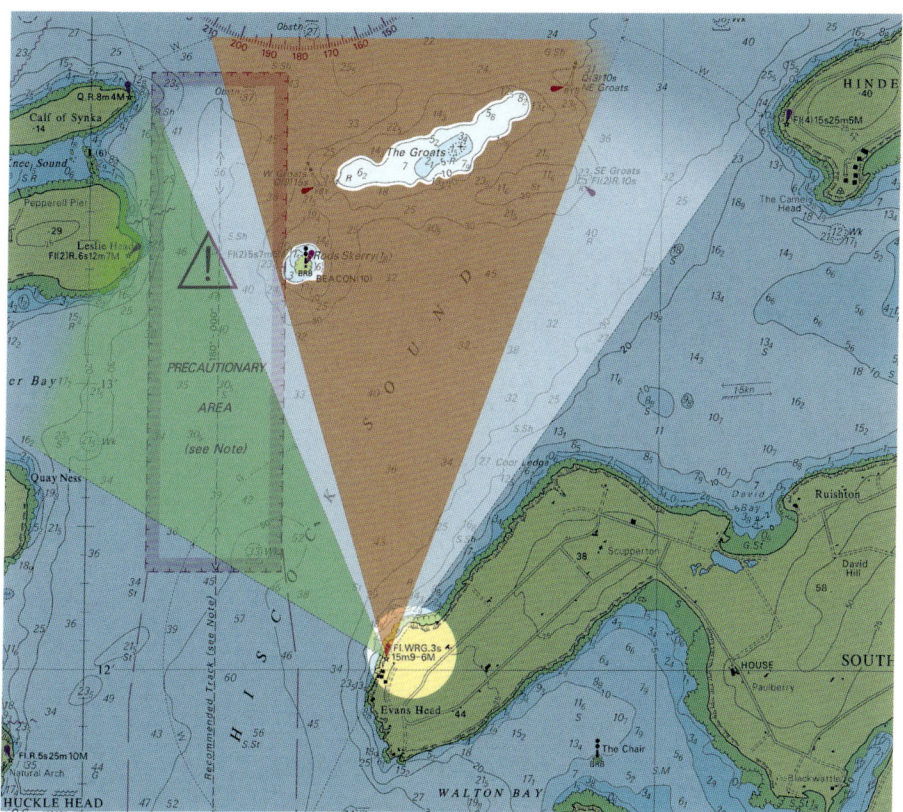

Sectored lights identify the safer zones to approach from and those from where it is unsafe to do so. Light characteristics may vary to identify different elements of the sector, such as when used as a directional light. The red sector in the illustration below highlights a danger area.

Lighthouses

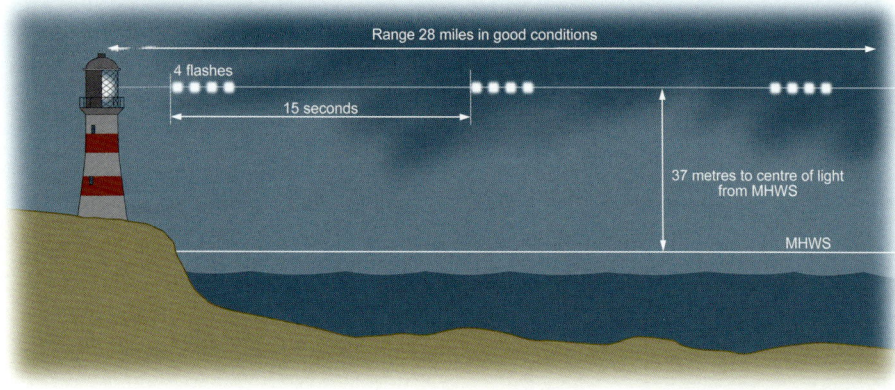

Fl(4)15s37m28M

Flashes **4** times every **15s**econds, height above MHWS **37m**etres, nominal range **28M**iles in <u>clear visibility</u>

The Nominal Range

This is a measure of the brightness of a light assuming that the atmospheric visibility is 10 miles. If the visibility is poor you may not see the light until you are much closer.

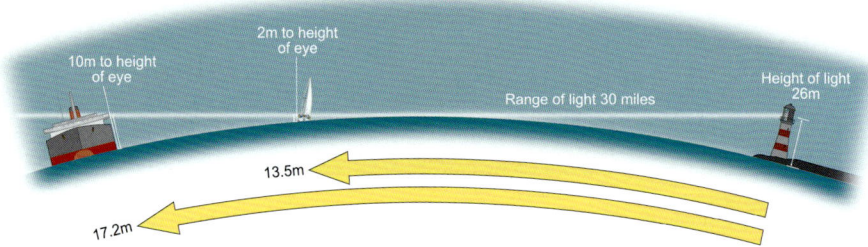

Nominal range does not account for the curvature of the earth. You won't be able to see a light unless you have a direct line of sight to it above the horizon.

Use the rising and dipping tables from an almanac to check at what range you will see the light.

Height of light		metres	1	2	3	Height of eye 5	6	7	8	9	10
metres	feet	feet	3	7	10	13	16	20	23	26	30	33
10	33		8·7	9·5	10·2	10·8	11·3	11·7	12·1	12·5	12·8	13·2
12	39		9·3	10·1	10·8	11·4	11·9	12·3	12·7	13·1	13·4	13·8
14	46		9·9	10·7	11·4	12·0	12·5	12·9	13·3	13·7	14·0	14·4
16	53		10·4	11·2	11·9	12·5	13·0	13·4	13·8	14·2	14·5	14·9
18	59		10·9	11·7	12·4	13·0	13·5	13·9	14·3	14·7	15·0	15·4
20	66		11·4	12·2	12·9	13·5	14·0	14·4	14·8	15·2	15·5	15·9
22	72		11·9	12·7	13·4	14·0	14·5	14·9	15·3	15·7	16·0	16·4
24	79		12·3	13·1	13·8	14·4	14·9	15·3	15·7	16·1	16·4	17·0
26	85		12·7	13·5	14·2	14·8	15·3	15·7	16·1	16·5	16·8	17·2
28	92		13·1	13·9	14·6	15·2	15·7	16·1	16·5	16·9	17·2	17·6

Leading Lights

The orientation of leading lights usually suggests which way you should turn to enter or leave harbour on the recommended ground track.

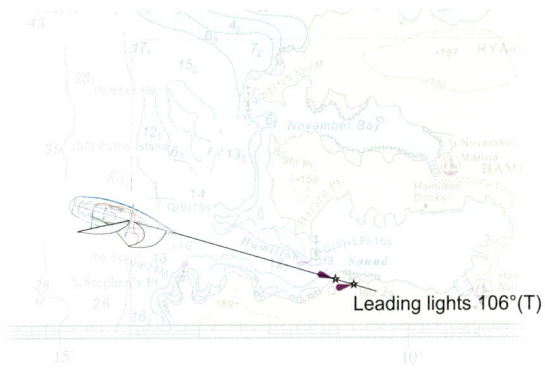

Leading lights guide you in and out of harbour.

Too far to starboard.　　　　　　On course.　　　　　　Too far to port.

Direction Lights

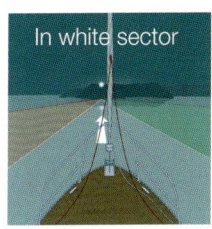 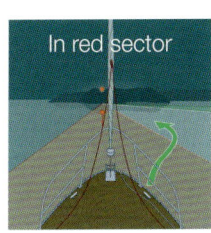 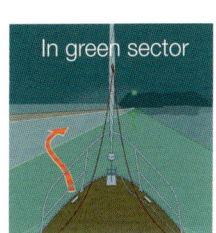

 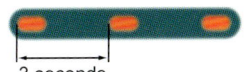 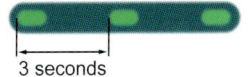

3 seconds　　　　　　3 seconds　　　　　　3 seconds

[101]

Pilotage

Pilotage is the art of inshore navigation typically when you have visual references to help you find your way along the coast and in and out of harbour. There may be lots of different hazards so good planning is essential.

Don't spend too much time down below – you will soon lose track of where you are and put yourself in danger. Making a good plan means you can navigate from on deck.

Things you might need to plan for:

Rocks.

Shoals and shallows.

Shipping channels.

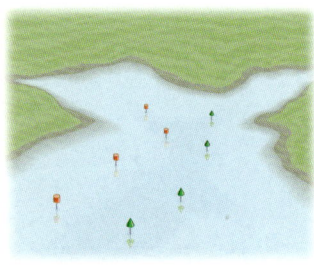

How an expanse of water changes at high water...

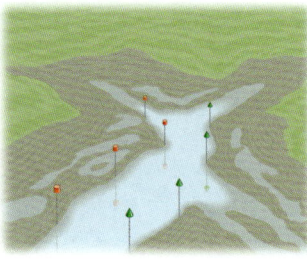

... and at low water.

Chain ferries.

Harbour byelaws e.g. small craft channels.

Speed restriction in channel.

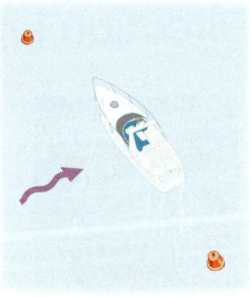

Effect of tide.

A different port may have a change of buoyage system. Here, it is IALA A buoyage.

PILOTAGE

International Port Traffic Signals

Serious emergency. Do not proceed.

Do not proceed. Waiting for lock.

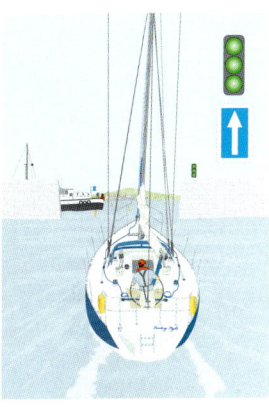

Proceed. One-way traffic.

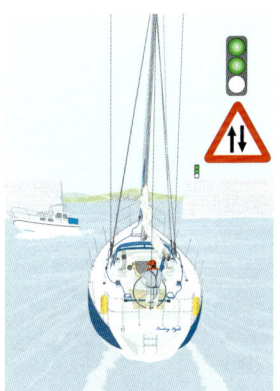

Proceed. Two-way traffic (e.g. lock freeflow).

Await orders to proceed.

Pilotage Techniques

Transits

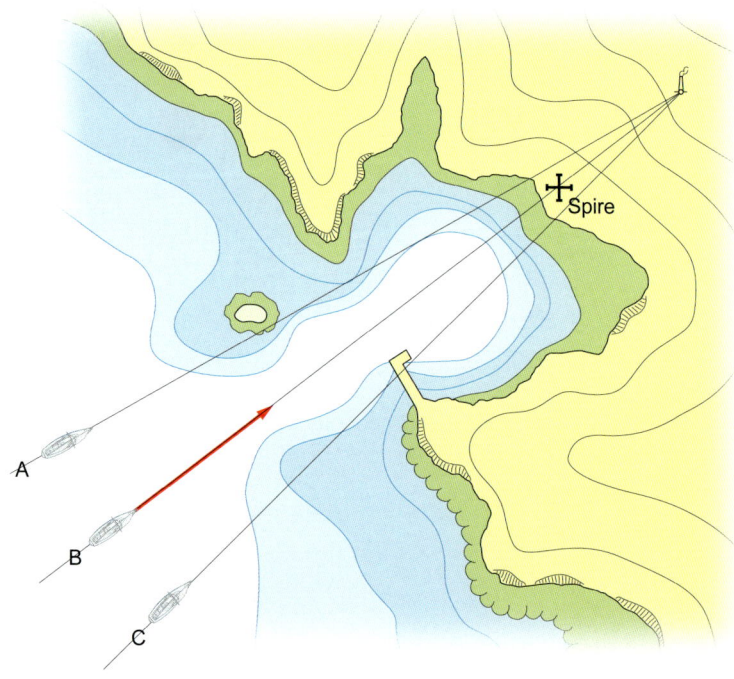

A = Too far to port

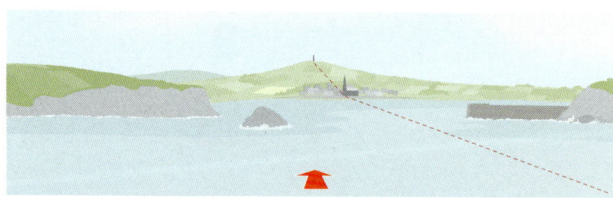

B = On track

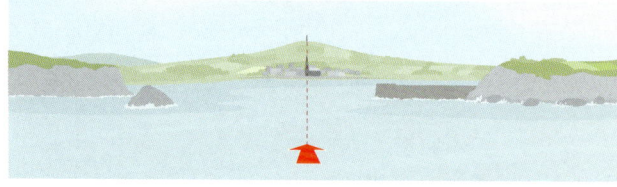

C = Too far to starboard

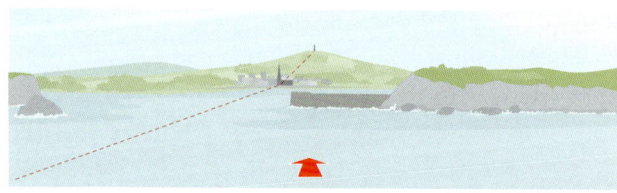

Contours

You can work out where you are when you cross a contour. They can be followed in poor visibility. Remember to allow for rise and fall of tide.

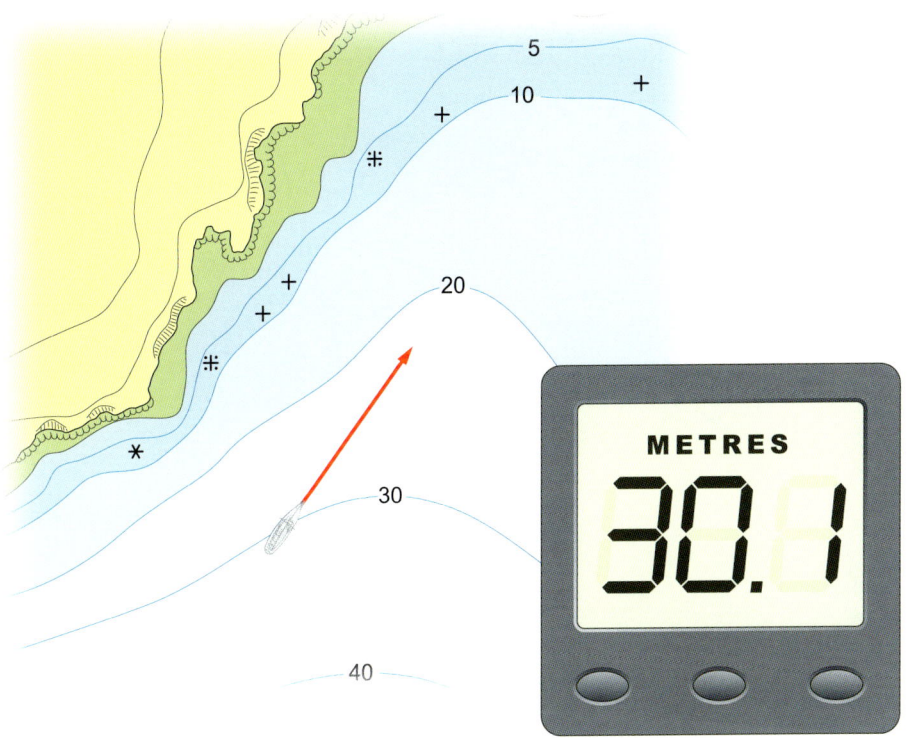

PILOTAGE TECHNIQUES

Clearing Bearing

You can go anywhere between the two bearings.

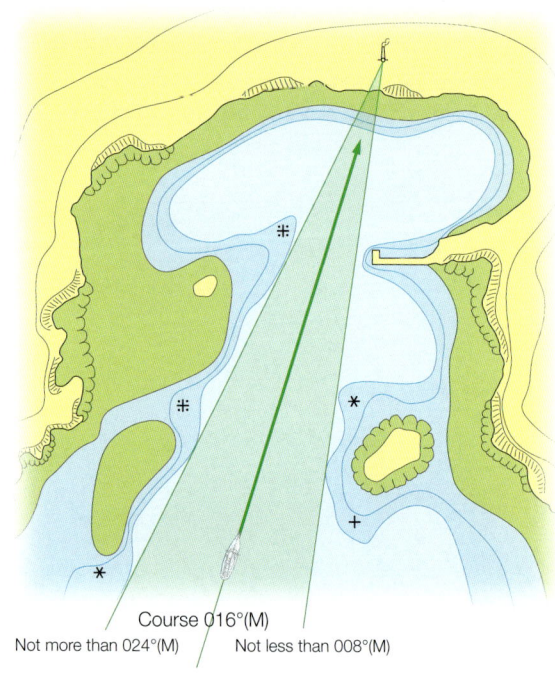

Course 016°(M)
Not more than 024°(M)   Not less than 008°(M)

Back Bearing

Course 335°(M)± to keep back bearing 155°(M)

PILOTAGE TECHNIQUES

Bearing & Distance

Work this out in advance so you know where to expect the next buoy.

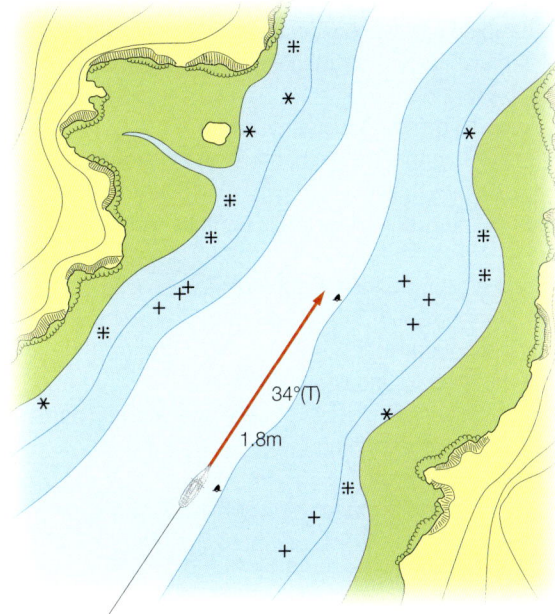

Course 34°(T). Distance between buoys 1.8 miles

Turning Points

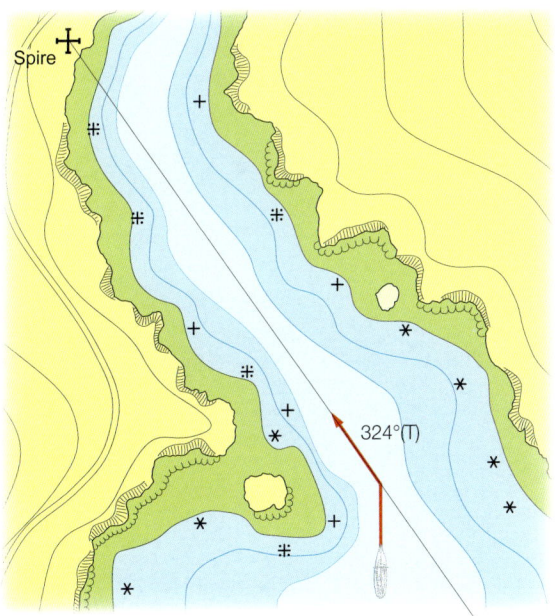

Turn when spire bears 324°(T)

[107]

Navigating in Pilotage Water

To navigate safely in congested inshore waters it is best to spend as much time as possible on deck. This means you are able to:

- keep an eye out for other vessels
- make sure that the yacht stays on the required ground track, using visual references.

The best way to achieve this is to make a plan in advance. For example:

Passage plan: Dunbarton to Endal Marina (see opposite page).

Information required:
- Tidal streams and tidal heights
- Is there sufficient depth of water to leave and arrive when we want to?
- Distance/journey time
- Hazards on route
- What aids to pilotage are available?
- VHF channels
- Port regulations.

Use chart, almanac and pilot book information to produce a pilotage plan.

By making a sketch you can extract the essential details of your plan to keep handy when on deck.

NAVIGATING IN PILOTAGE WATER

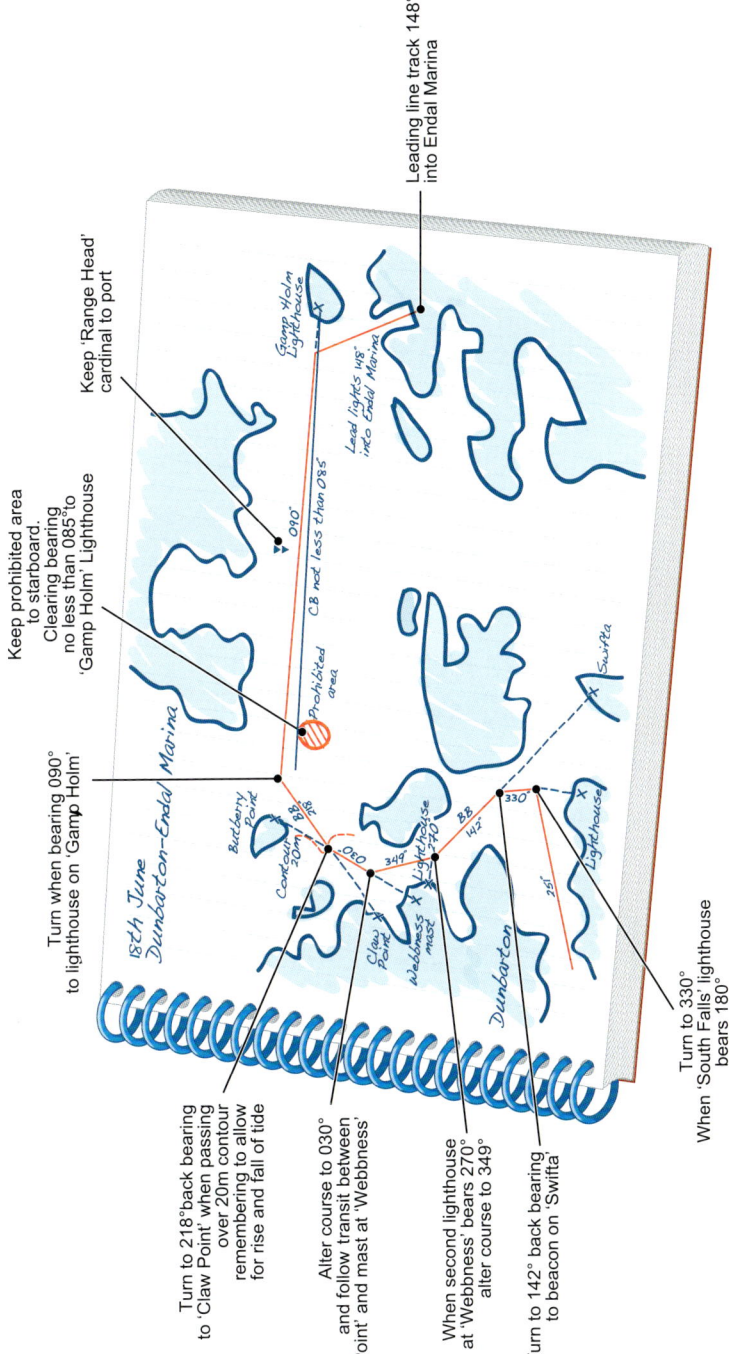

[109]

Anchoring

Delta
Good holding-to-weight ratio. Designed to stay on bow roller for self-launching.

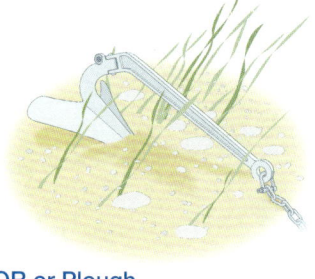

CQR or Plough
Good holding-to-weight ratio. Hard to stow and moving parts can capsize.

Bruce
Good holding-to-weight ratio. Awkward to store in a small anchor locker.

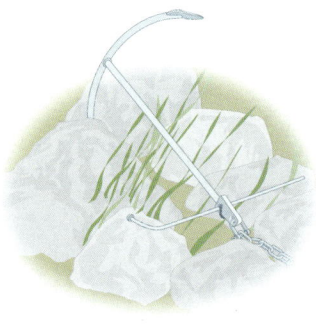

Fisherman's
Traditional type. Good for rocky and weedy bottoms. Awkward to stow and poor holding power in sand and mud.

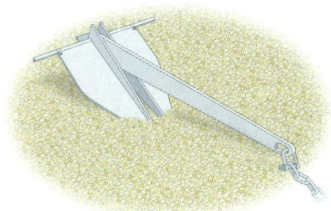

Danforth
Good holding-to-weight ratio. Stows flat. Can be hard to break out of mud.

Grapnel
Normally quite light. Awkward to stow unless it's a collapsing model. Good in coral or rock. Poor in mud, clay or sand. Better suited to a tender than as a vessel's main anchor.

ANCHORING

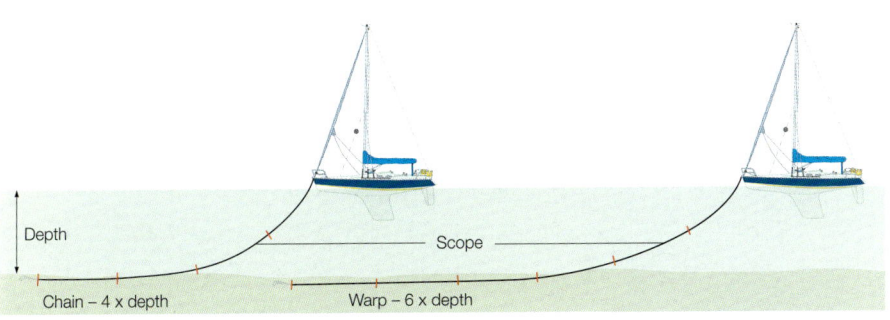

Scope
The scope of chain or warp you need depends on the maximum depth of water you expect during your stay.

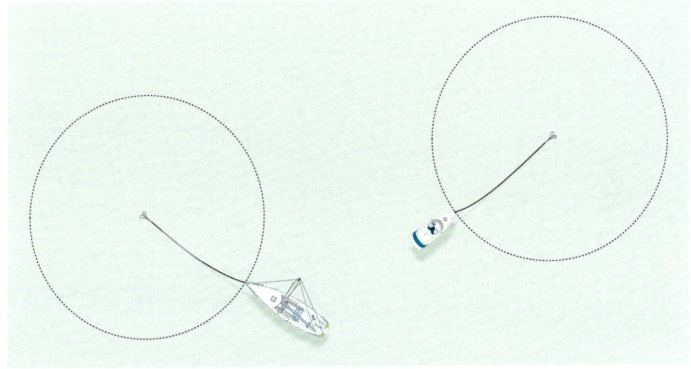

Always allow enough swinging room to account for wind and tide. Bear in mind that light/flat-bottomed boats will lie differently to deeper draught/low windage boats.

Anchoring in a narrow creek or channel.

Anchoring in heavy weather. Set two anchors at 45 degrees to each other.

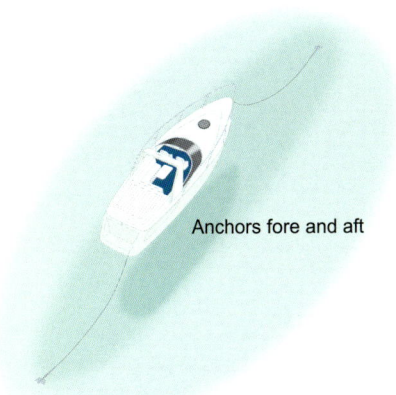

Anchors fore and aft

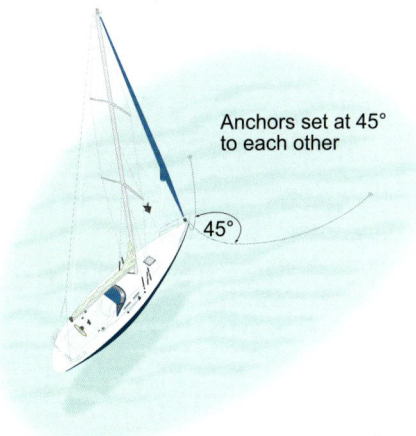

Anchors set at 45° to each other

45°

ANCHORING

Selecting an Anchor Berth

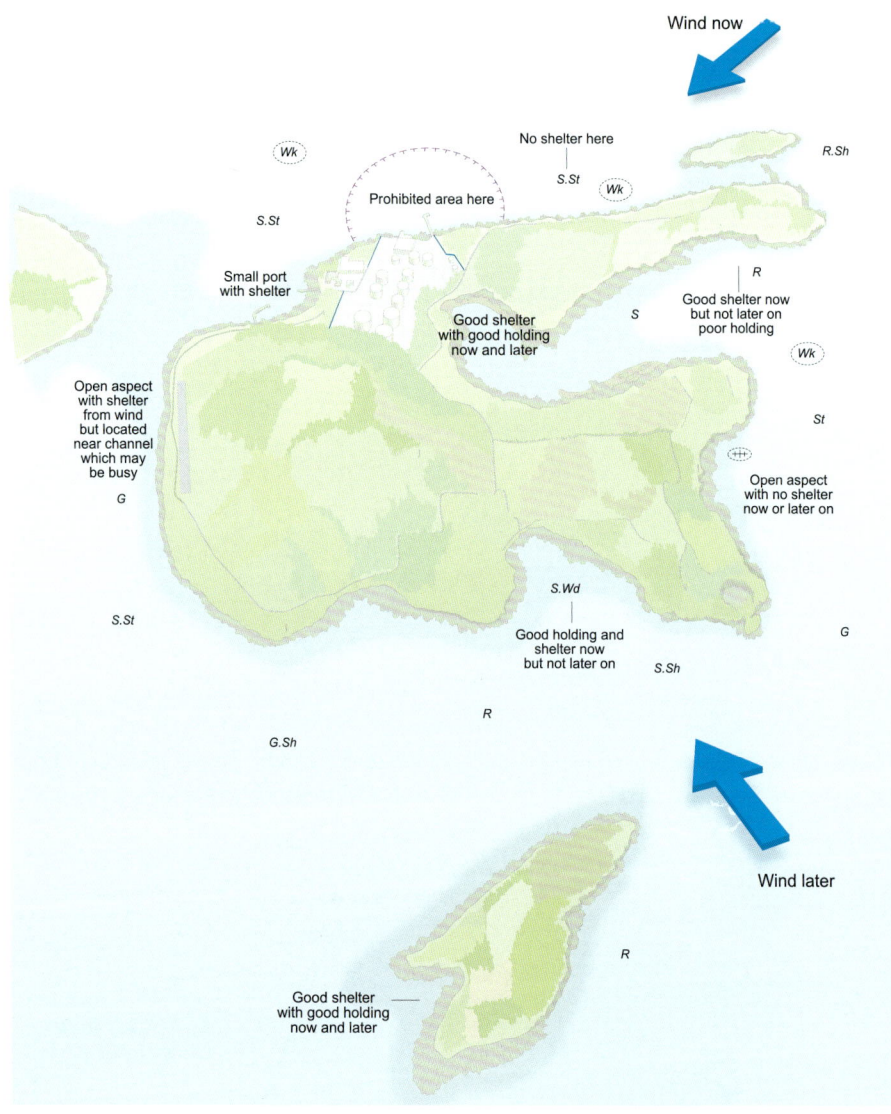

Some points to consider:
- Shelter from wind/swell/tidal stream
- Tidal rise and fall
- The nature of the seabed
- Swinging room – other boats/hazards etc.

Circulation

In very simple terms: hot air at the equator rises and is replaced by cooler air moving in from elsewhere.

In reality the situation is more complex because of the unequal distribution of land and water.

When air moves away from the equator to the poles it is deflected east.

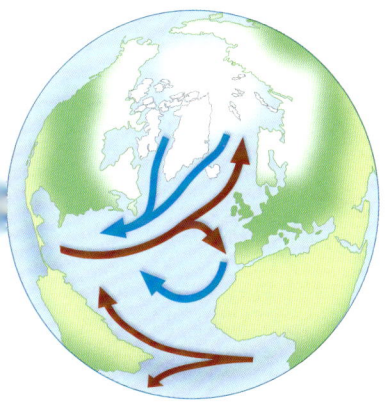

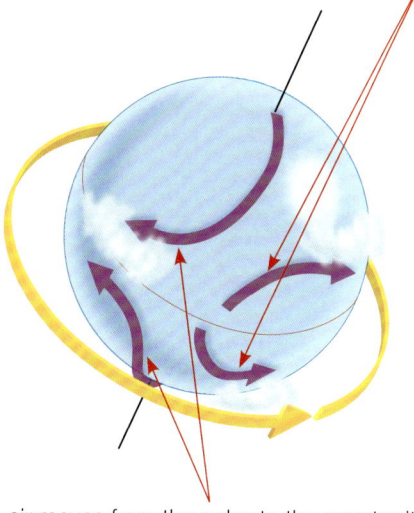

The oceans act like giant storage heaters. Ocean currents move warm and cold water to different parts of the globe.

When air moves from the poles to the equator it is deflected to the west.

TIP: Winds bend to the right in the Northern Hemisphere, and to the left in the Southern Hemisphere.

CIRCULATION

A combination of all these effects leads to complex weather patterns.

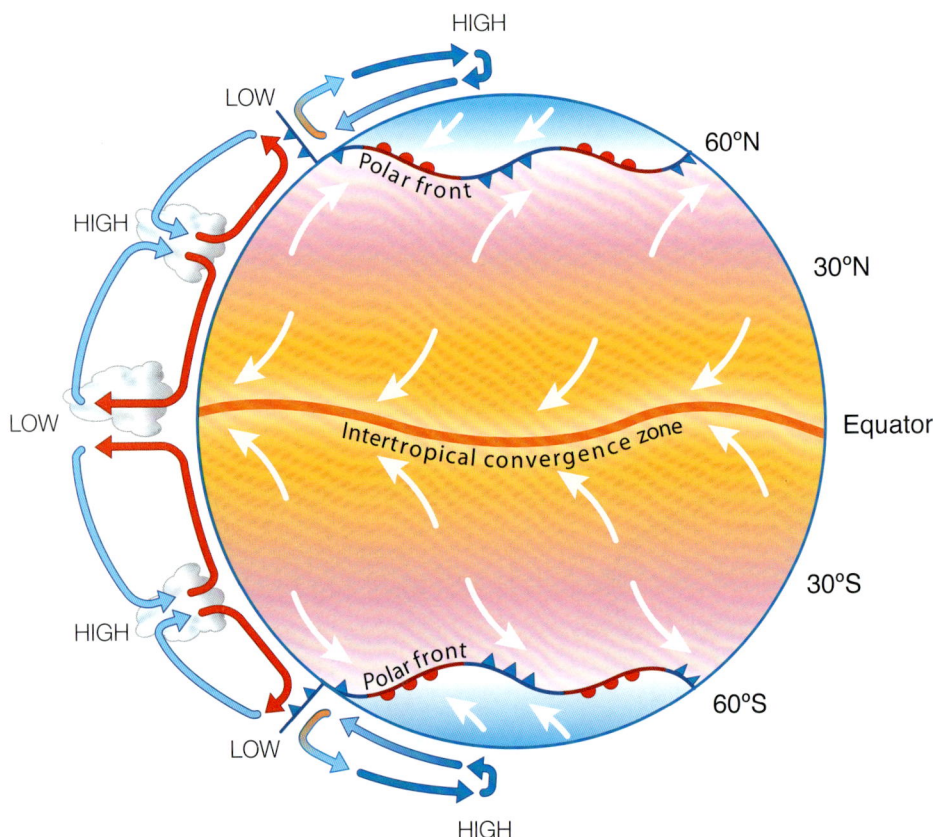

CIRCULATION

Seasonal variations also affect the prevailing weather.

Weather Systems

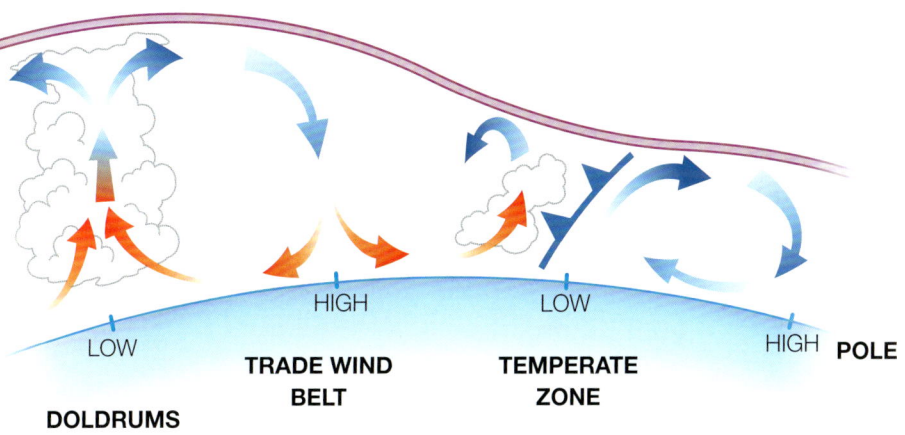

These produce distinctive weather patterns around the globe, such as the light airs in the doldrums, the trade winds used by old sailing ships, and temperate zones dominated by depressions.

Depressions (Northern Hemisphere)

Depressions form at the barrier of cold polar air and warmer tropical air.

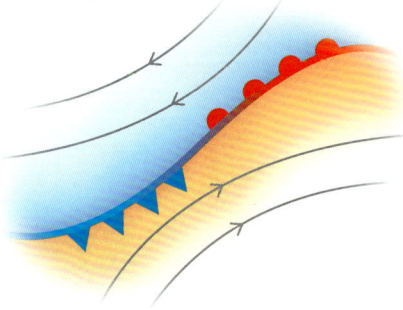

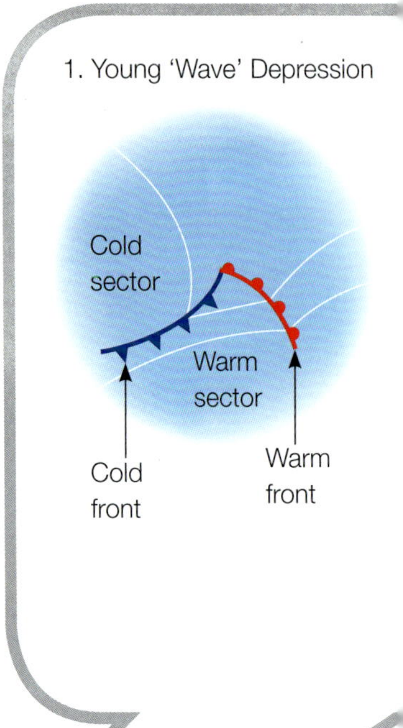

1. Young 'Wave' Depression

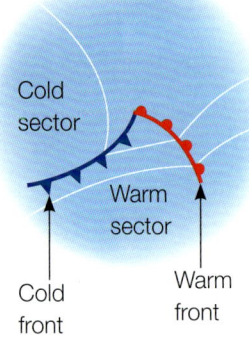

Cold sector
Warm sector
Cold front
Warm front

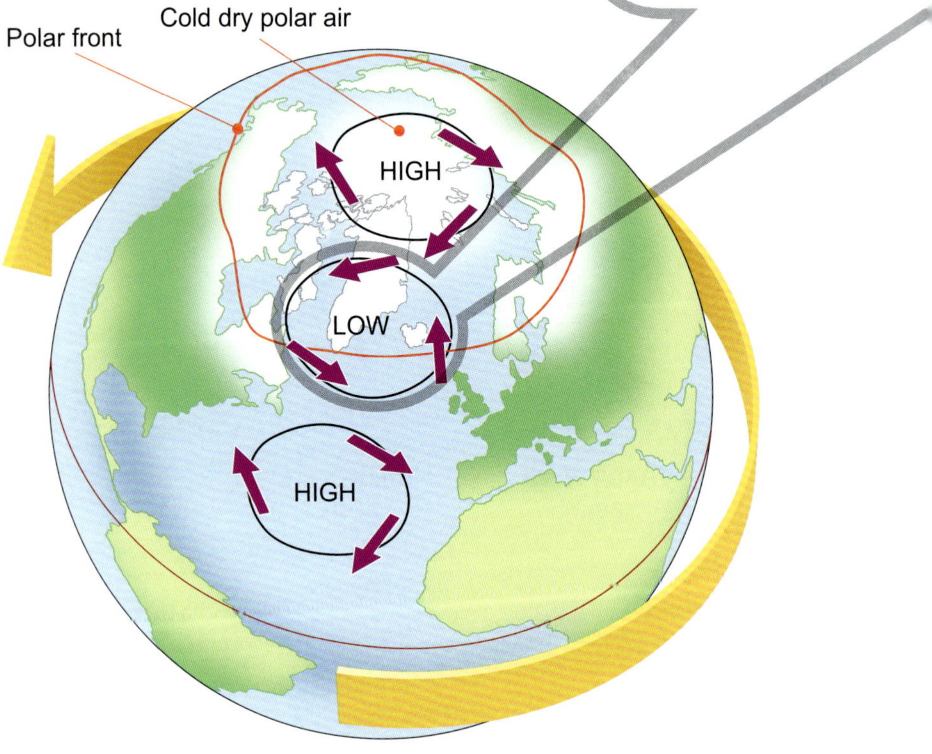

Polar front
Cold dry polar air
HIGH
LOW
HIGH

DEPRESSIONS (NORTHERN HEMISPHERE)

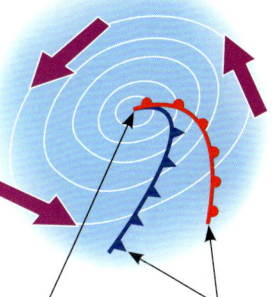

2. Active Deepening Depression

Pressure at the centre deepens

Cold front starts to catch up warm front as warm air rises

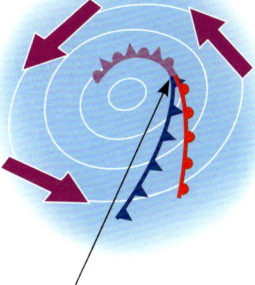

3. Maturing Depression

Warm and cold fronts meet up to make occluded front

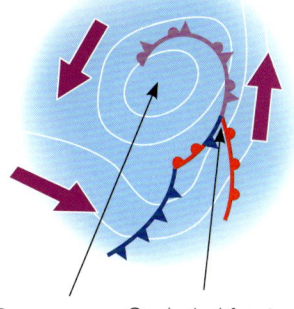

4. Mature Depression

Pressure at the centre fills

Occluded front 'zips up' as fronts meet and warm air has risen above cold air

Isobars are lines of equal atmospheric pressure that are used to depict weather systems. They are used in a similar way to contours on a land map.

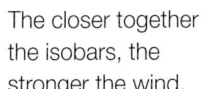

The closer together the isobars, the stronger the wind.

Buy's Ballots Law shows that when you face the wind in the Northern Hemisphere, the low is on your right.

Air tries to flow from a high-pressure area to a low-pressure area but is deflected by the Coriolis effect to blow along the isobars. The wind measured from the alignment and distance apart of the isobars is known as the pressure gradient wind.

Depressions (Southern Hemisphere)

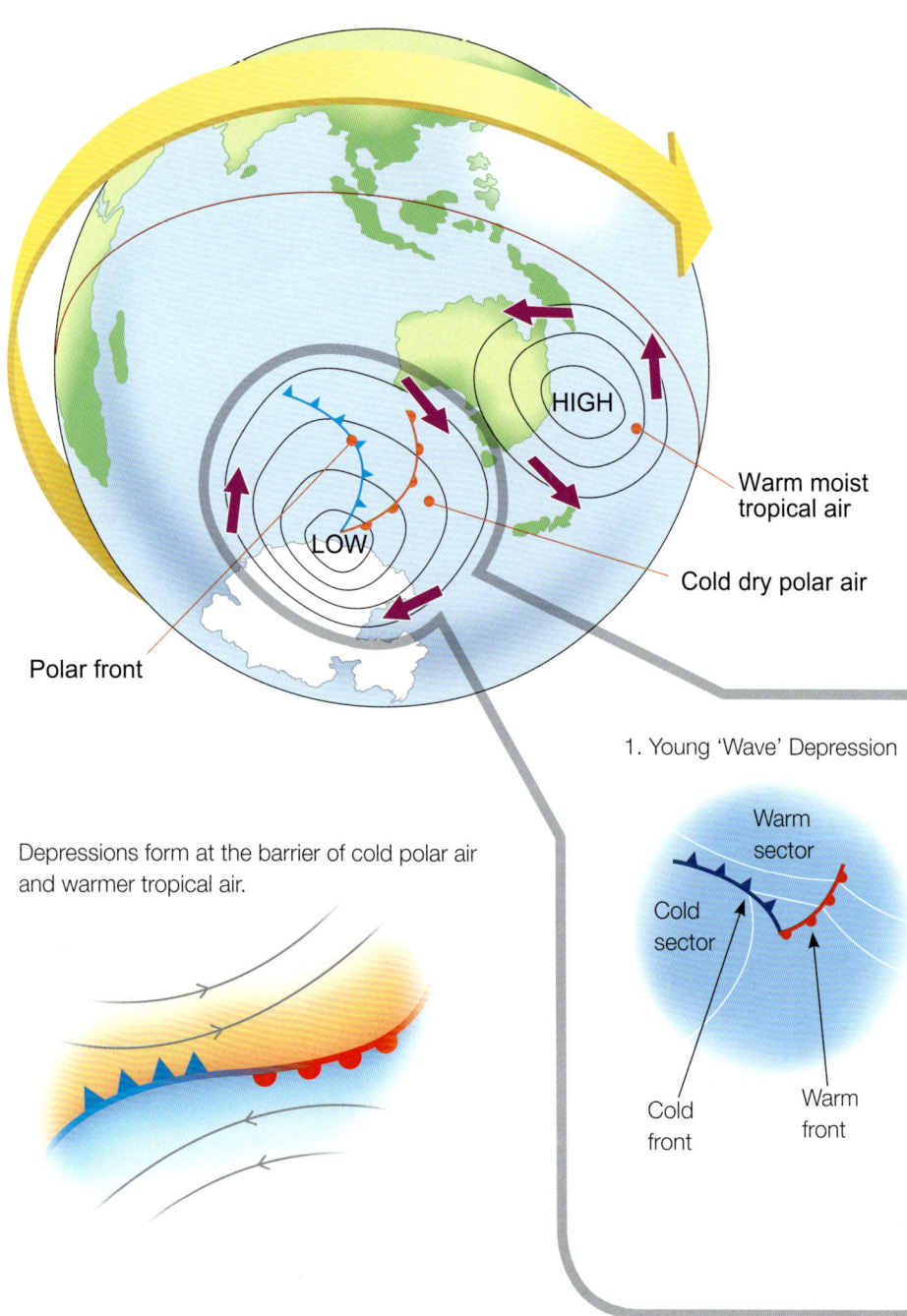

DEPRESSIONS (SOUTHERN HEMISPHERE)

Isobars are lines of equal atmospheric pressure that are used to depict weather systems. They are used in a similar way to contours on a land map.

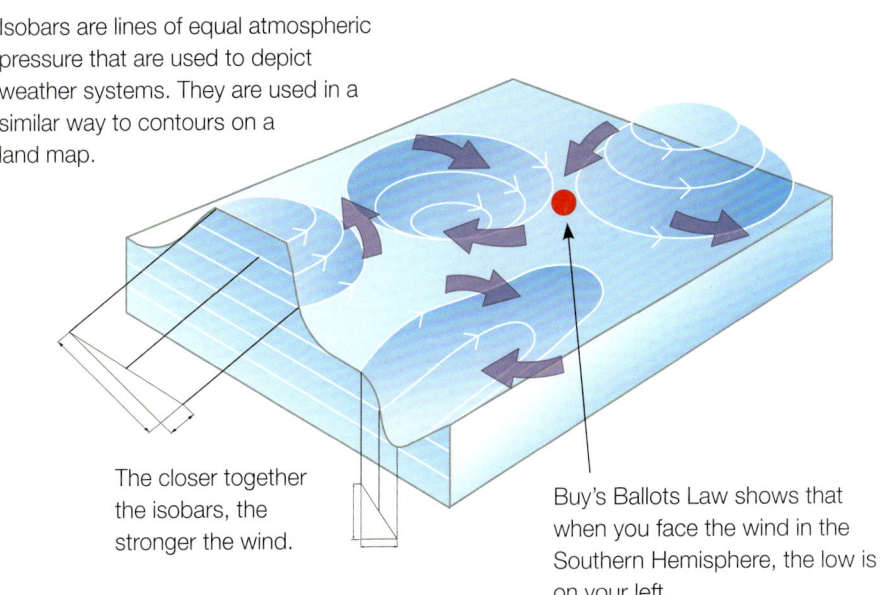

The closer together the isobars, the stronger the wind.

Buy's Ballots Law shows that when you face the wind in the Southern Hemisphere, the low is on your left.

Air tries to flow from a high-pressure area to a low-pressure area but is deflected by the Coriolis effect to blow along the isobars. The wind measured from the alignment and distance apart of the isobars is known as the pressure gradient wind.

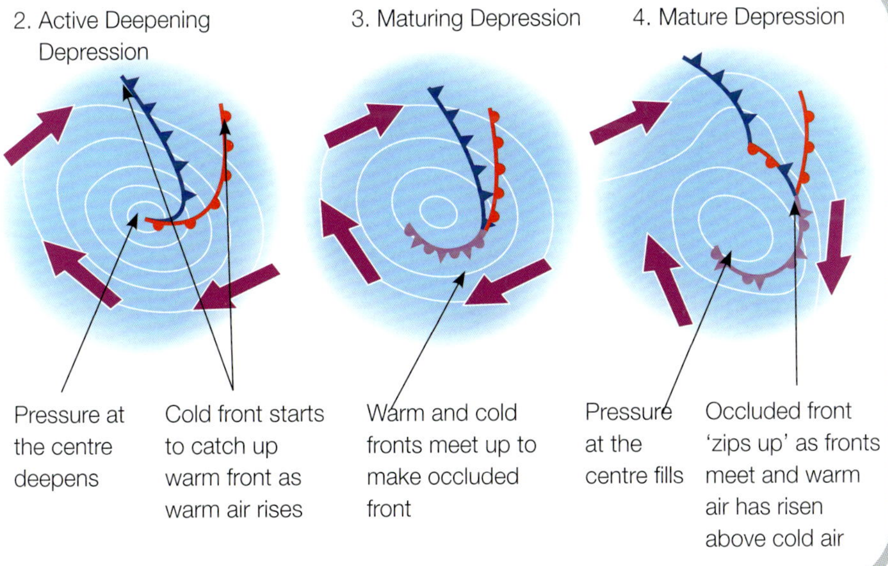

2. Active Deepening Depression

Pressure at the centre deepens

Cold front starts to catch up warm front as warm air rises

3. Maturing Depression

Warm and cold fronts meet up to make occluded front

4. Mature Depression

Pressure at the centre fills

Occluded front 'zips up' as fronts meet and warm air has risen above cold air

Passage of a Depression

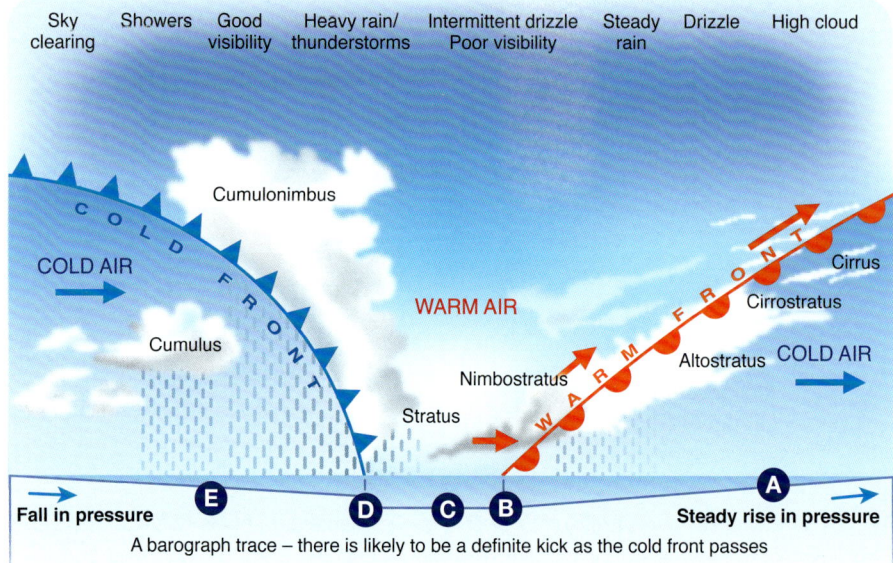

A barograph trace – there is likely to be a definite kick as the cold front passes

A Warm Front Approaching

- Wind backs and increases in the Southern Hemisphere
- Wind veers and increases in the Northern Hemisphere
- Pressure falls
- Cloud base descends and thickens, and rain becomes heavier
- Visibility deteriorates in rain
- Temperature begins to increase as you near the warm front.

B Warm Front Passes

- Wind veers in the Northern Hemisphere
- Wind backs in the Southern Hemisphere
- Pressure stops falling
- Rain turns to drizzle
- Visibility deteriorates
- Humidity increases as temperature rises.

C In the Warm Sector

- Wind direction steady
- Pressure steady
- Patchy drizzle or light rain
- Visibility moderate or poor. Fog likely
- Humid.

D Cold Front Passes

- In the Northern Hemisphere, wind veers often with squall
- In the Southern Hemisphere, wind backs often with squall
- Pressure rises sharply
- Heavy rain, possibly hail and thunder
- Visibility poor in rain
- Temperature begins to drop.

E Behind the Cold Front

- Wind direction steady, stronger, and gusty
- Pressure rises then levels
- Temperature lower
- Sunshine and showers
- Visibility good except in showers.

PASSAGE OF A DEPRESSION

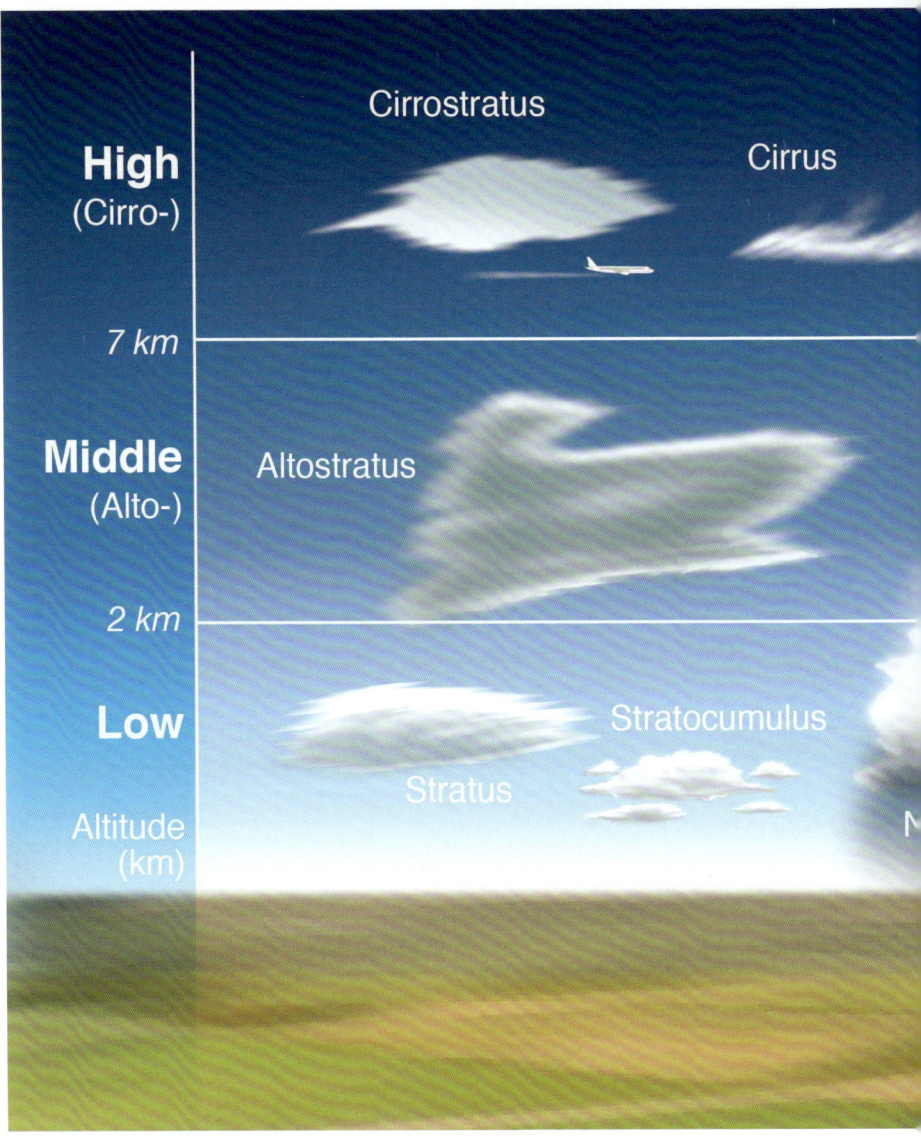

Clouds

Cirro/us – high level, wispy clouds (6,000–12,000m).

Alto – Mid-level clouds (2,000–6,000m).

Nimbo/us – dark rain-bearing clouds (low or mid-level only).

PASSAGE OF A DEPRESSION

Strato/us – layered clouds.

Cumulo/us – fluffy clouds.

Combinations are possible, e.g. cirrostratus – a high-level layer or stratocumulus – low-level fluffy clouds becoming layered.

High-pressure Systems

Northern Hemisphere

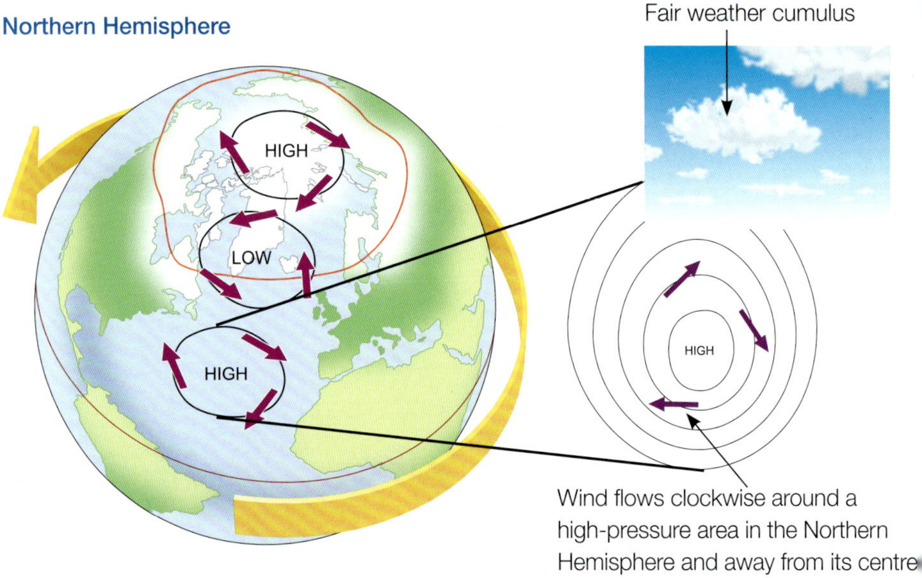
Fair weather cumulus
HIGH
LOW
HIGH
HIGH
Wind flows clockwise around a high-pressure area in the Northern Hemisphere and away from its centre

A high-pressure area or anticyclone is usually associated with fine, settled weather and light winds. However, you might experience locally strong winds which have been funnelled by coasts and mountains.

Southern Hemisphere

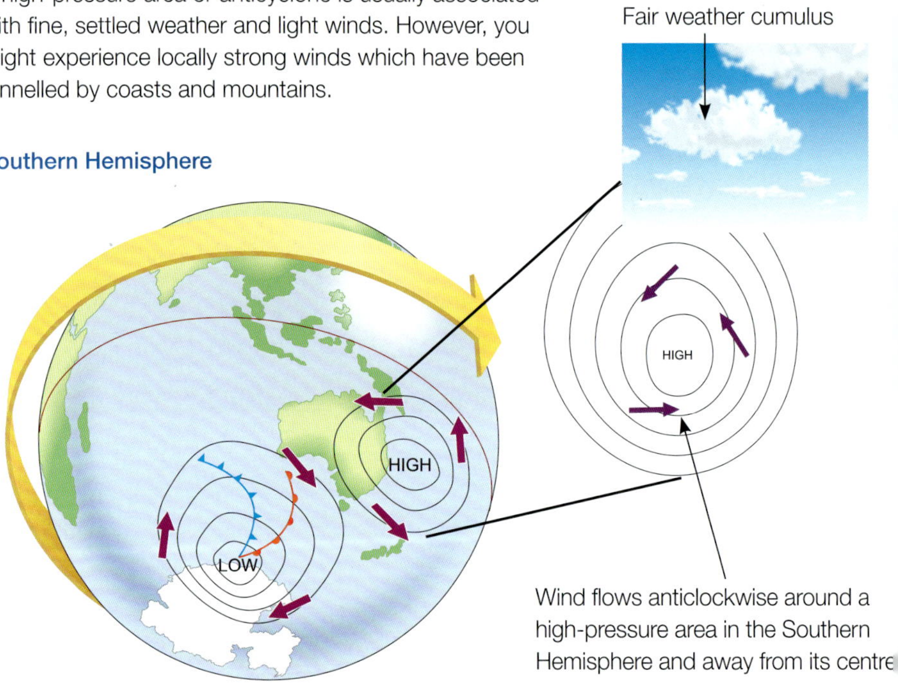
Fair weather cumulus
HIGH
LOW
HIGH
Wind flows anticlockwise around a high-pressure area in the Southern Hemisphere and away from its centre

Air Masses

Arctic
Very cold dry air moving over a warmer sea. Unstable.

Polar Maritime
Cold air moving over a warmer sea. An unstable air flow bringing squalls and very good visibility (except in the squalls).

Polar Continental
Summer: warm air over a cool sea. Hazy and stable. From a north-easterly direction the long sea track over the North Sea can mean fog.
Winter: cold or very cold air. From the north-east the cold air passing over the warm sea can bring showers or snow flurries.

Tropical Maritime
Warm, moist air moving over a colder sea. Expect poor visibility in a stable air flow.

Tropical Continental
The UK's hottest air mass. Hazy and often stable, although when combined with the right conditions thunderstorms can occur.

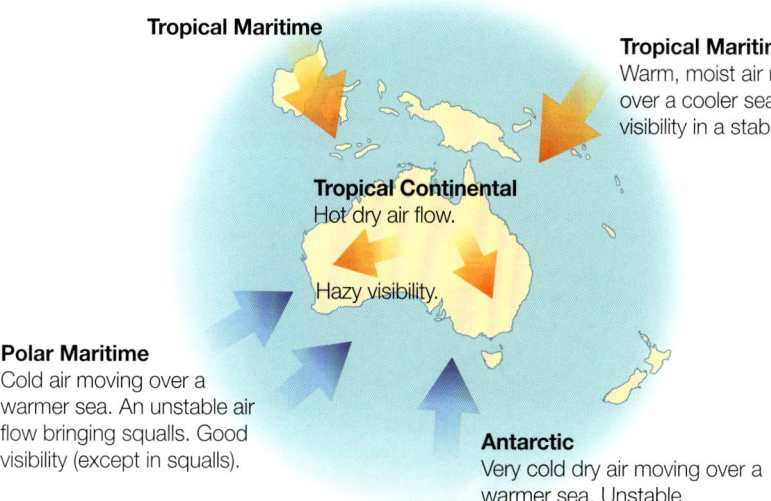

Tropical Maritime

Tropical Maritime
Warm, moist air moving over a cooler sea. Moderate visibility in a stable air flow.

Tropical Continental
Hot dry air flow.
Hazy visibility.

Polar Maritime
Cold air moving over a warmer sea. An unstable air flow bringing squalls. Good visibility (except in squalls).

Antarctic
Very cold dry air moving over a warmer sea. Unstable.

Local Land Effects

Sea Breeze

A sea breeze is likely to develop in fair weather and light to moderate offshore wind. Warm air rises over land. It then cools, descends, and blows onshore. The wind is up to force 4 in strength.

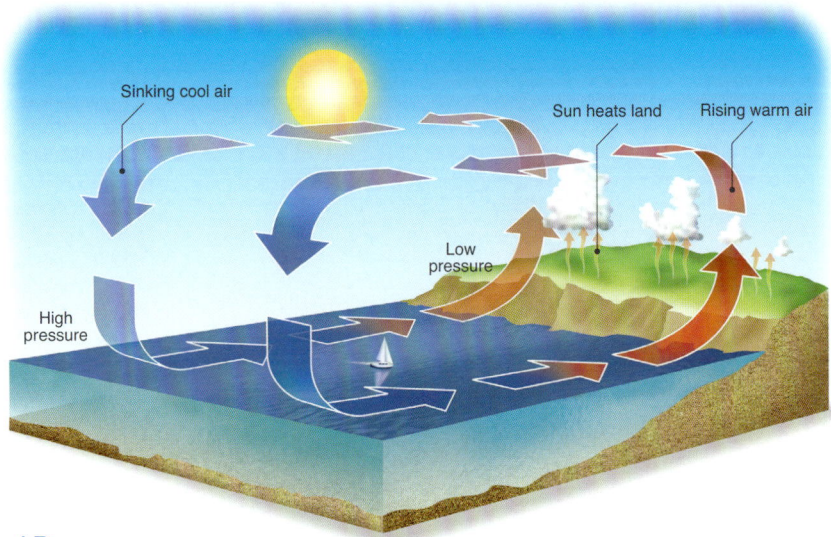

Land Breeze

Land breeze occurs on a clear night when the air cools over land and flows downhill and out to sea, particularly from river estuaries. The wind is usually no more than force 2–3, except near mountains.

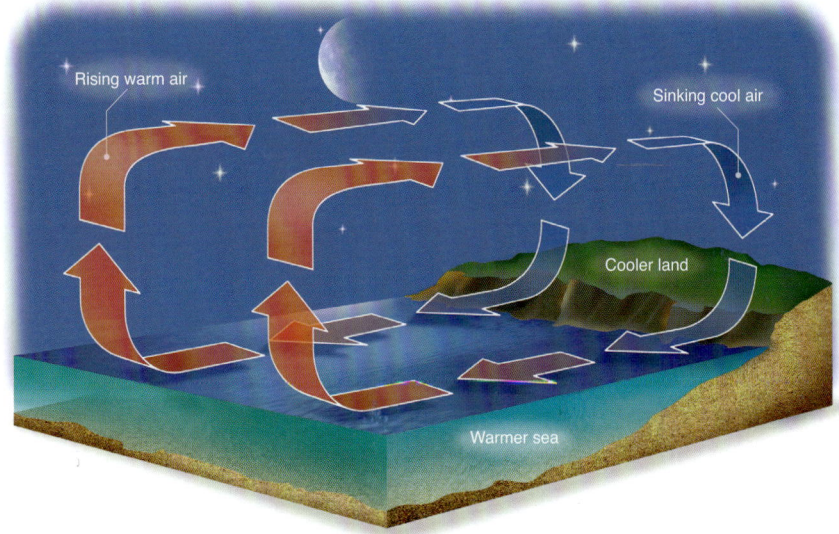

LOCAL LAND EFFECTS

Katabatic Wind

In areas with high land, strong offshore winds can develop as cold mountain air rolls downhill. These can be very dangerous winds as they may occur without warning.

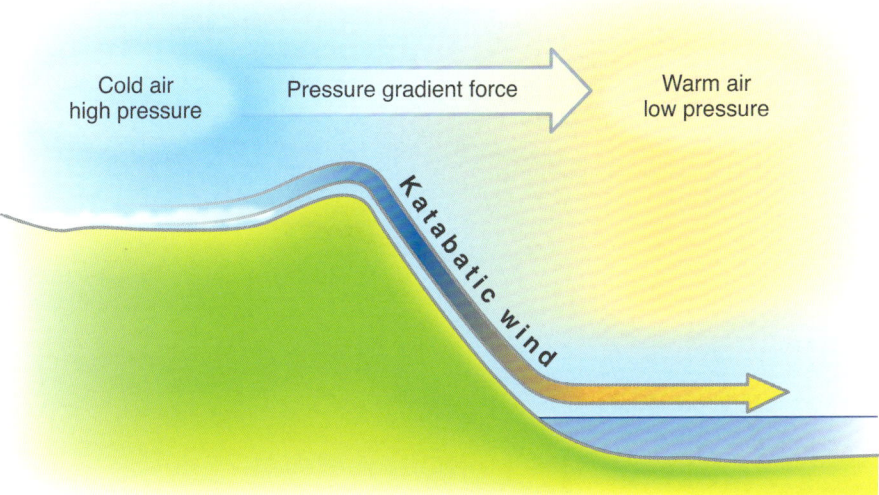

Radiation Fog

Radiation or land fog usually occurs in settled weather in autumn/winter. Land cools down quickly at night. Moisture condenses and forms fog over land, which will drift out to sea on the land breeze.

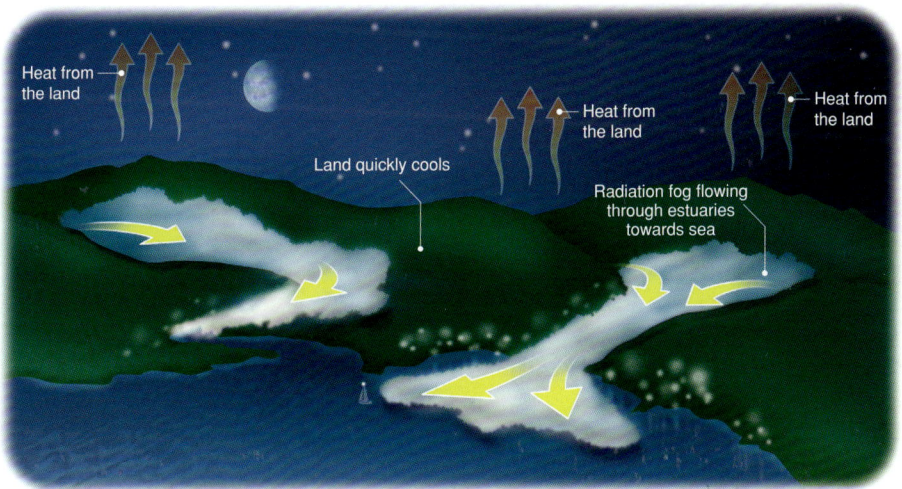

LOCAL LAND EFFECTS

Advection Fog

Advection or sea fog forms when warm, moist air exists above a colder sea. The sun will not burn off sea fog. The fog will clear with a change of air mass to something colder and dryer.

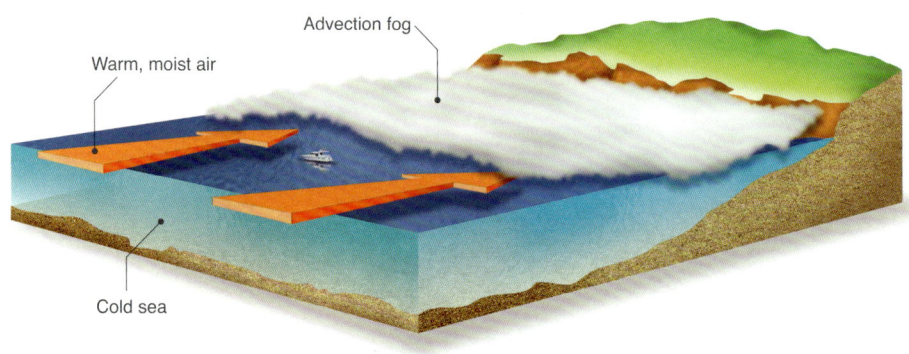

Offshore & Onshore Winds

Wind blowing offshore can be fluky in direction and strength, especially when blowing off trees, buildings, cliffs, etc.

In onshore winds the sea state can be worse further inshore as the water shallows. Lee shore can be dangerous in strong winds.

LOCAL LAND EFFECTS

Land Effects due to Friction

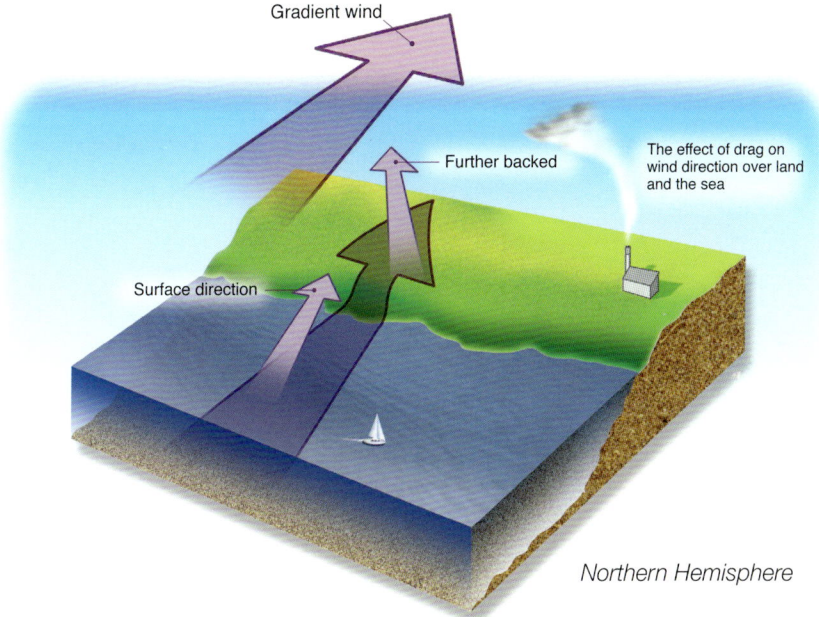

Northern Hemisphere

As wind slows due to friction it changes direction. It backs in the Northern Hemisphere and veers in the Southern. As the friction is greater over land the size of the backing/veering is greater.

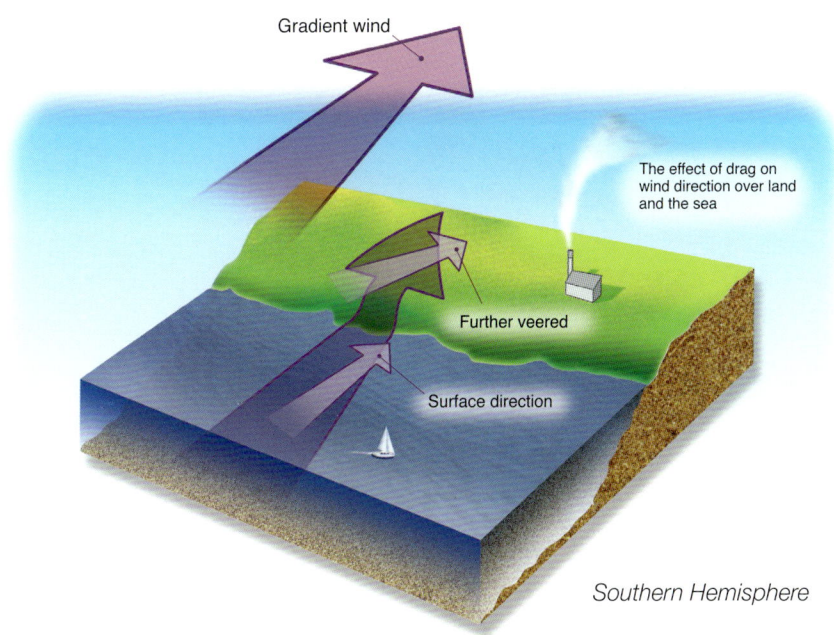

Southern Hemisphere

LOCAL LAND EFFECTS

Convergent and Divergent Winds (Northern Hemisphere)

The backing effect can cause stronger or lighter winds when the wind is along a coast.

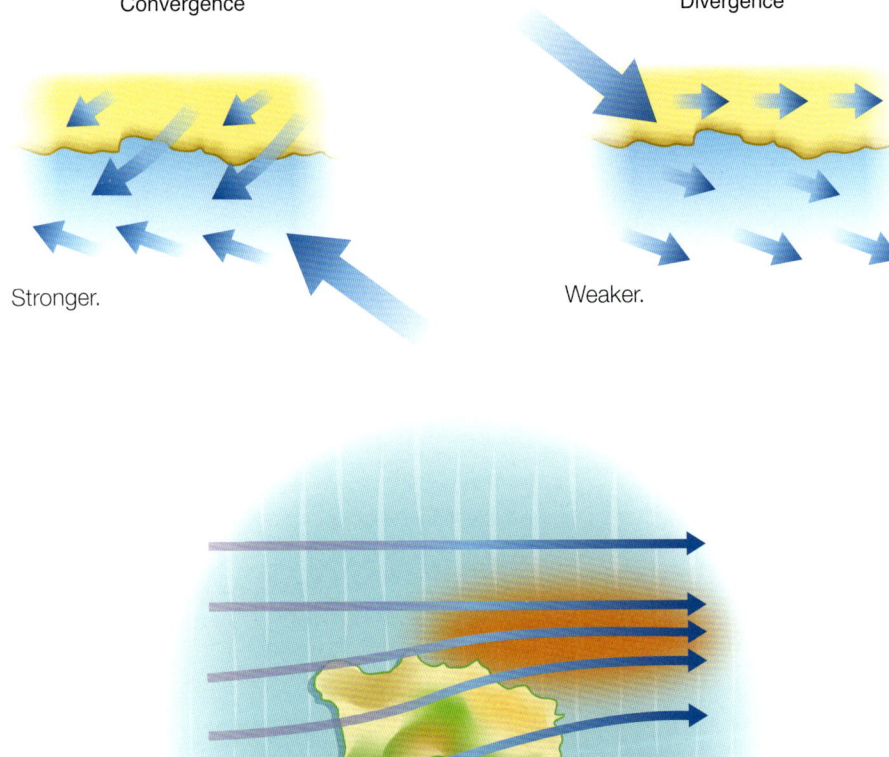

Convergence — Stronger.

Divergence — Weaker.

If wind crosses an island, convergence and divergence can make one side stronger.

LOCAL LAND EFFECTS

Convergent and Divergent Winds (Southern Hemisphere)

The veering effect can cause stronger or lighter winds when the wind is along a coast.

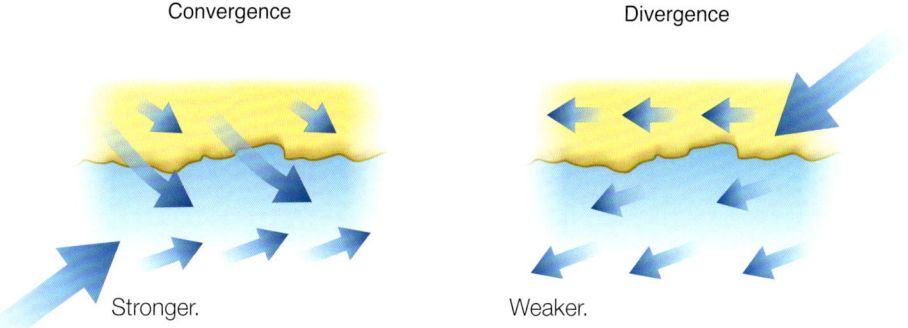

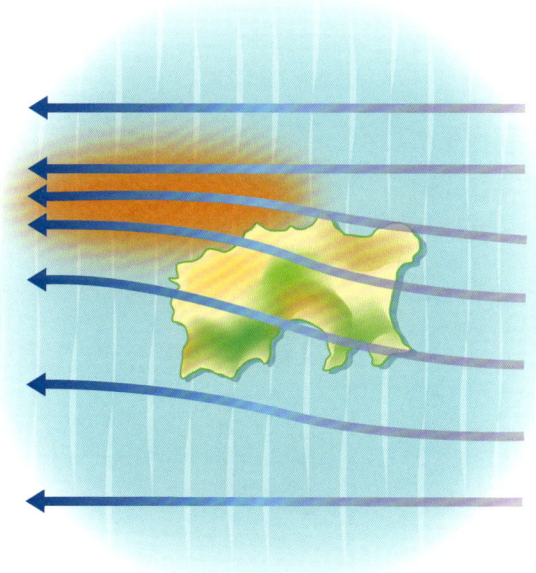

If wind crosses an island, convergence and divergence can make one side stronger.

Weather Forecasts

Shipping Forecast Areas
Get to know your local forecast area.

There are many different ways to obtain a forecast.

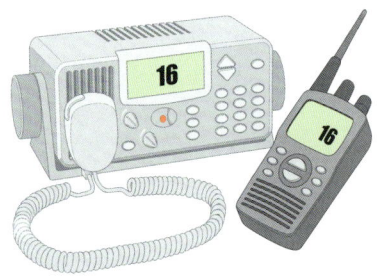

Marine safety information broadcasts on VHF by the Coastguard.

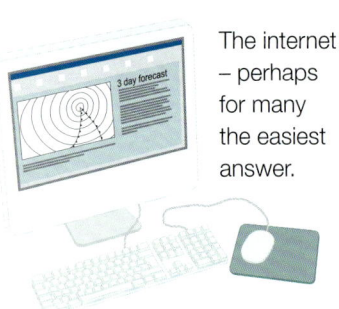

The internet – perhaps for many the easiest answer.

Many harbour and marina offices post a forecast.

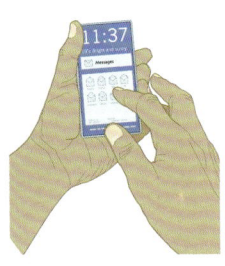

Smartphone apps.

Recorded forecasts by phone.

National and local radio stations.

WEATHER FORECASTS

TERMS USED IN FORECASTS

Gale warnings	If average wind is expected to be F8 or more (34–40 knots), or gusts 43–51 knots. Severe gale: Winds of force 9 (41–47 knots) or gusts reaching 52–60 knots. Storm: Winds of force 10 (48–55 knots) or gusts reaching 61–68 knots. Violent storm: Winds of force 11 (56–63 knots) or gusts of 69 knots or more. Hurricane force: Winds of force 12 (64 knots or more).
Strong wind warnings	If average wind is expected to be F6 or F7. F6 is often called a 'yachtsman's gale'.
Imminent	Within 6 hours of time of issue of warning.
Soon	Within 6–12 hours of time of issue of warning.
Later	More than 12 hours from time of issue of warning.
Visibility	Good = greater than 5 miles. Moderate = between 2–5 miles. Poor = 1,000m to 2 miles. Very Poor = less than 1,000m.
Fair	No significant precipitation.
Backing	Wind changing in an anticlockwise direction e.g. NW to SW.
Veering	Wind changing in a clockwise direction e.g. NE to SE.
General synopsis	How and where the weather systems are moving.
Sea states	Smooth = wave height 0.2–0.5m. Slight = wave height 0.5–1.25m. Moderate = wave height 1.25m–2.5m. Rough = wave height 2.5m–4m. Very rough = wave height 4m–6m. High = wave height 6m–9m. Very high = wave height 9m–14m. Phenomenal = wave height more than 14m.
Movement of pressure systems	Slowly = moving at less than 15 knots. Steadily = moving at 15–25 knots. Rather quickly = moving at 25–35 knots. Rapidly = moving at 35–45 knots. Very rapidly = moving at more than 45 knots.
Pressure tendency in station reports	Rising (or falling) more slowly = pressure rising (or falling) at a progressively slower rate through the preceding three hours. Rising (or falling) slowly = pressure change of 0.1 to 1.5 hPa in the preceding three hours. Rising (or falling) = pressure change of 1.6 to 3.5 hPa in the preceding three hours. Rising (or falling) quickly = pressure change of 3.6 to 6.0 hPa in the preceding three hours. Rising (or falling) very rapidly = Pressure change of more than 6.0 hPa in the preceding three hours Now rising (or falling) = Pressure has been falling (rising) or steady in the preceding three hours, but at the time of observation was definitely rising (or falling). Note: For those more familiar with the millibar, 1 hPa = 1 mbar

The Beaufort Scale

1. Light airs. 1–3 knots. Ripples. Sail = drifting conditions. Power = fast planing conditions.

2. Light breeze. 4–6 knots. Small wavelets. Sail = full mainsail and large genoa. Power = fast planing conditions.

3. Gentle breeze. 7–10 knots. Occasional crests. Sail = full sail. Power = fast planing conditions.

4. Moderate. 11–16 knots. Frequent white horses. Sail = reduce headsail size. Power = may have to slow down if wind against tide.

5. Fresh breeze. 17–21 knots. Moderate waves, many white crests. Sail = reef mainsail. Power = reduce speed to prevent slamming when going upwind.

6. Strong breeze. 22–27 knots. Large waves, white foam crests. Sail = reef main and reduce headsail. Power = displacement speed.

7. Near gale. 28–33 knots. Sea heaps up, spray, breaking waves, foam blows in streaks. Sail = deep reefed main, small jib. Power = displacement speed.

8. Gale. 34–40 knots. Moderately high waves, breaking crests. Sail = deep reefed main, storm jib. Power = displacement speed, stem waves.

9. Severe gale. 41–47 knots, High waves, spray affects visibility. Sail = trysail and storm jib. Power = displacement speed, stern waves.

10. Storm. 48–55 knots. Very high waves, long breaking crests. Survival conditions.

11. Violent storm. 56–63 knots. Exceptionally high seas with continuously breaking waves seriously affecting visibility. Survival tactics.

12. Hurricane. 64 knots and above. Exceptionally high seas with continuously breaking waves seriously affecting visibility. Survival tactics.

Passage Planning

1. How far is it?
2. What time do we need to arrive?
3. What is the weather forecast?

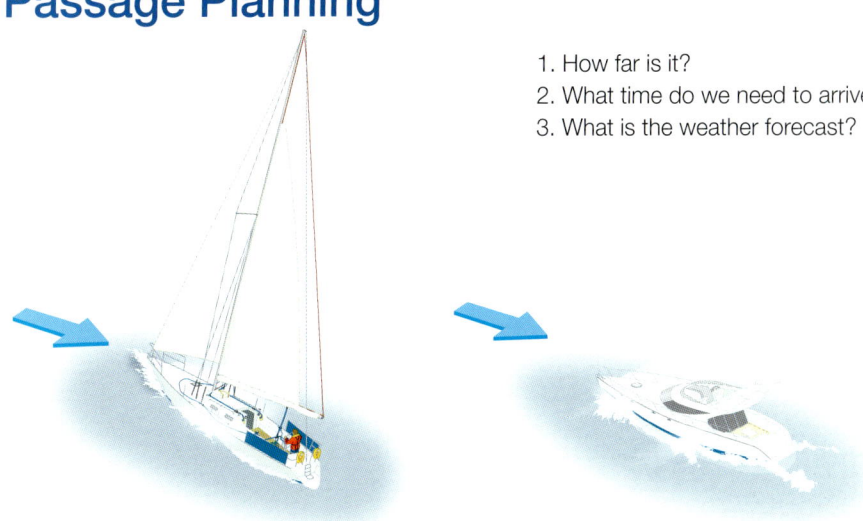

4. How long will the passage take? Progress upwind can be slow and uncomfortable.

You can steer a more direct course downwind and make good progress.

Boat speed 18 knots / Distance 60 miles = 3.5 hours.
Boat speed 6 knots / Distance 60 miles = 10 hours.
Will any of these hours be in darkness?

PASSAGE PLANNING

Tidal Gates

5. The fastest passage in a sailing boat is with a favourable tide. This could mean rougher water. Motor yachts are faster in a flat sea, even if this means a passage against the tide.

6. What allowances must be made for tide?

7. What hazards will be encountered en route?

8. Prepare pilotage plan for departure and entry, preparing for arrival in darkness.

9. Will you be able to sustain your course with any changes in wind direction?

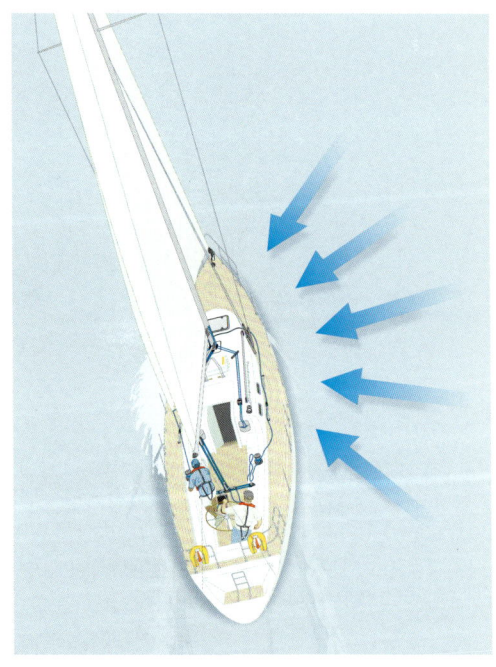

PASSAGE PLANNING

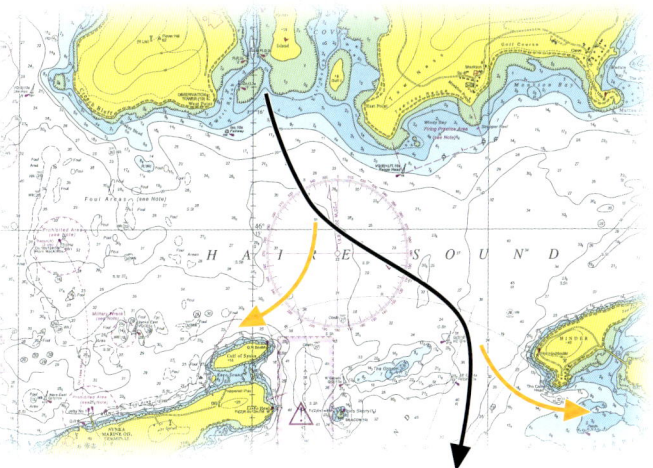

10. Determine suitable places of refuge.

11. Have you enough fuel?

12. As skipper, when do you need to be on deck? Arrange watch systems around crew strengths.

13. Is the passage within the limits of you, your crew, and your boat?

Principles of Voyage Planning

Appraisal
Suitability of the vessel, particularly its material state, and limitations imposed by draught, air draft, stability, and range.

Crew numbers and ability.

Paperwork for equipment or personnel carried. e.g. radio licences, certificates of competence, or customs.

Appropriate charts and publications including:
- Tide tables
- Tidal Stream data
- Sailing directions, almanacs or pilot books
- Appropriate scale planning and detail charts
- Navigational instruments and aids to navigation.

Weather forecasts and expected patterns or features for that area.

Marine communication such as Maritime Safety Broadcasts, harbour communication channels.

Volume of traffic likely to be encountered throughout the voyage.

Planning
A detailed voyage or passage plan should be prepared, covering the entire voyage from berth to berth, including those in pilotage waters.

Factors to be considered include:
- Identifying the intended route on appropriate scale charts/electronic charts
- Identifying any dangers or areas to avoid
- Any restrictions on routes taken and reporting systems such as harbour controls requiring notification of entry/departure
- MARPOL consideration.

Speed limits.

Depth of water and tidal heights (or expected) with regard to under-keel clearance.

The method and frequency of position fixing, including primary and secondary options, and the indication of areas where accuracy of position fixing is critical.

Contingency plans for alternative action to place the vessel in deep water or proceed to a port of refuge or safe anchorage.

Execution
Prior to executing the plan the following information should be updated with any changed or updated information:
- Condition of the vessel's navigational equipment
- Review ETAs at critical points for tide heights and flow
- Update meteorological information including periods of low visibility
- Clarify daytime versus night-time passing of danger points, and any effect this may have on position fixing accuracy.

Monitoring
The progress of the vessel in accordance with the plan should be closely and continuously monitored to ensure early indication of a need for variation.

Special Situations

Restricted Visibility

It is not advisable to set out in fog, especially if you don't have a radar set. However, if you are caught out:

Fix your position.

Hoist your radar reflector.

Sound foghorn at intervals of no more than two minutes (—) or (—··). Listen.

SPECIAL SITUATIONS

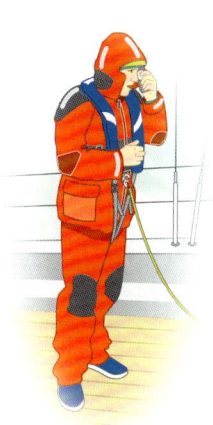

Muster crew on deck in lifejackets.

Listen on port frequency to check for commercial traffic.

If you have radar, keep an experienced person on constant watch.

1. Get out of busy shipping lanes or areas.

2. If possible, use depth and radar to help navigate into a harbour or safe anchorage.

SPECIAL SITUATIONS
Heavy Weather

For most coastal trips you should aim to avoid heavy weather, but when offshore you may have to deal with it. When preparing for heavy weather:
- Check that all gear is securely stowed, particularly heavy gear
- Secure hatches, lockers, and any washboards that will prevent water entering the vessel
- Consider navigational options to avoid lee shores or other dangers
- Rig jackstays or safety lines if they are not already fitted
- Ensure all on deck are clipped on, including those in the cockpit
- Close deck ventilators which will allow water below
- Check cockpit drains are clear
- Prepare storm sails such as a trysail or storm jib, or move reefing pennants to deep reef points.

SPECIAL SITUATIONS

Man Overboard

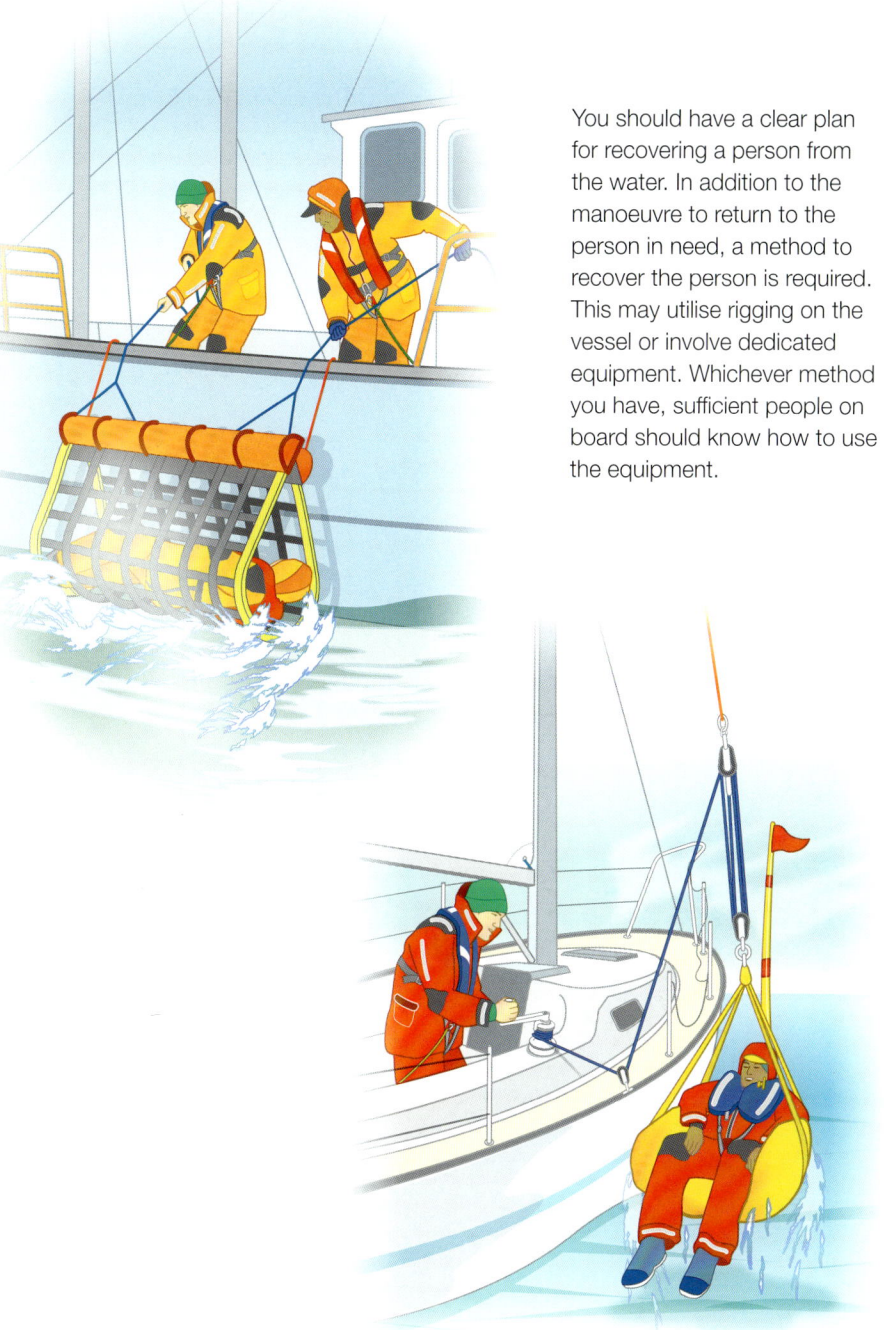

You should have a clear plan for recovering a person from the water. In addition to the manoeuvre to return to the person in need, a method to recover the person is required. This may utilise rigging on the vessel or involve dedicated equipment. Whichever method you have, sufficient people on board should know how to use the equipment.

SPECIAL SITUATIONS

Grounding & Collisions

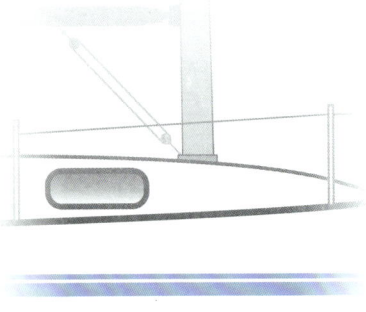

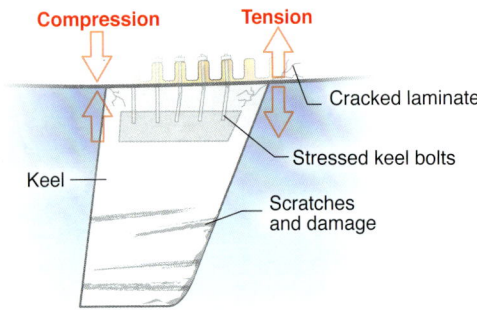

If your vessel is involved in a collision or grounding it may sustain serious damage. The damage may not always be in obvious places.

A yacht grounding while under way may have compression and tension cracking to the frames or hull.

After a collision or grounding you should check and monitor your bilges for water ingress. If water is entering you should try to locate the source, and consider action such as reducing sail area, decreasing speed, and making for the nearest safe port.

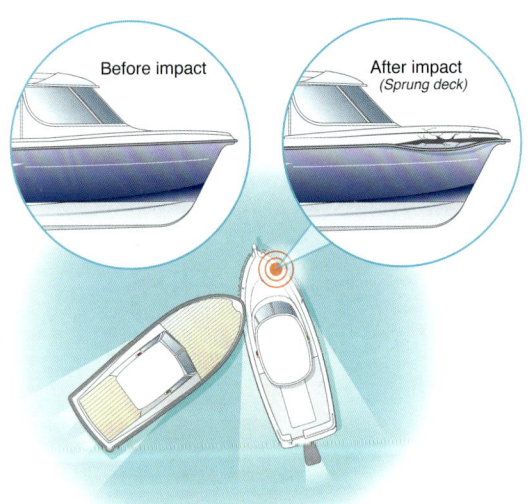

Collisions may result in sprung joints and damage away from the initial point of impact due to flexing or twisting of the hull.